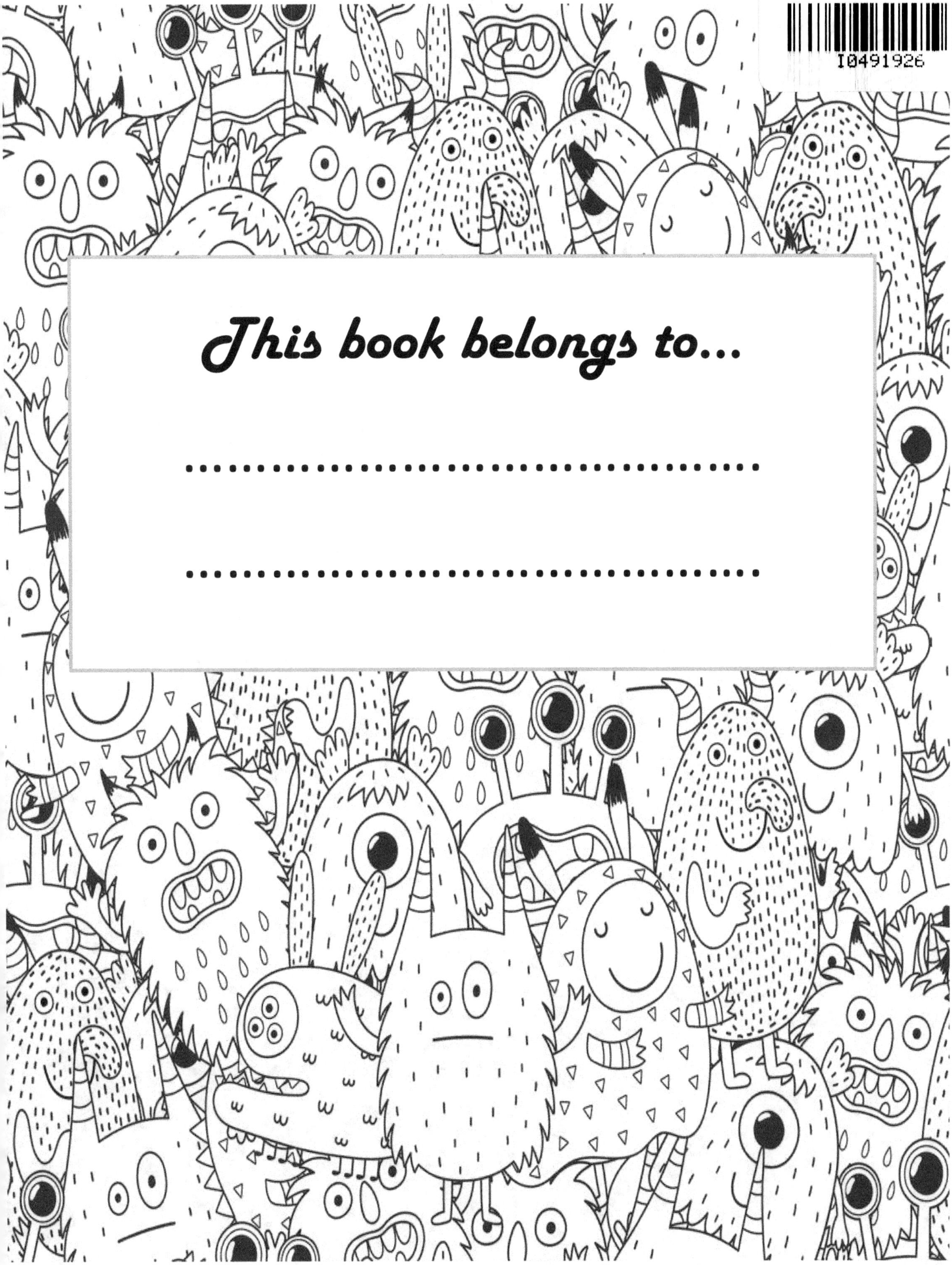
This book belongs to...
....
....

Small preview of what's inside

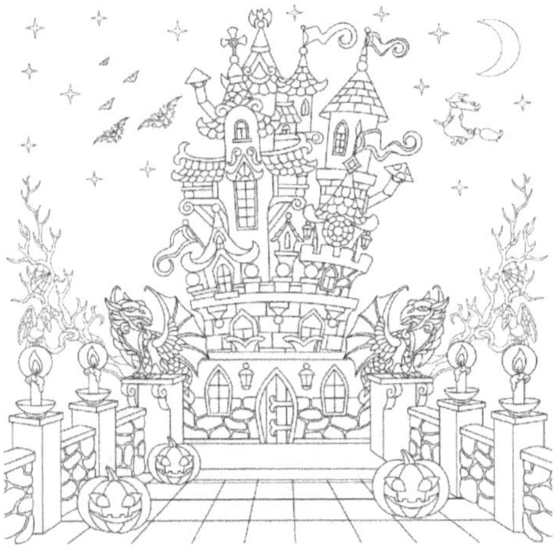

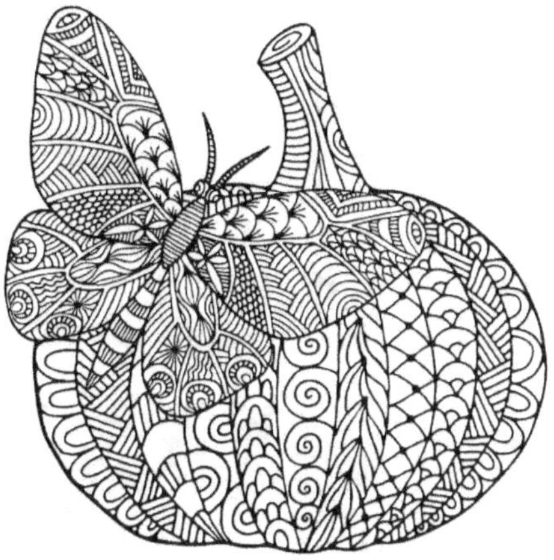

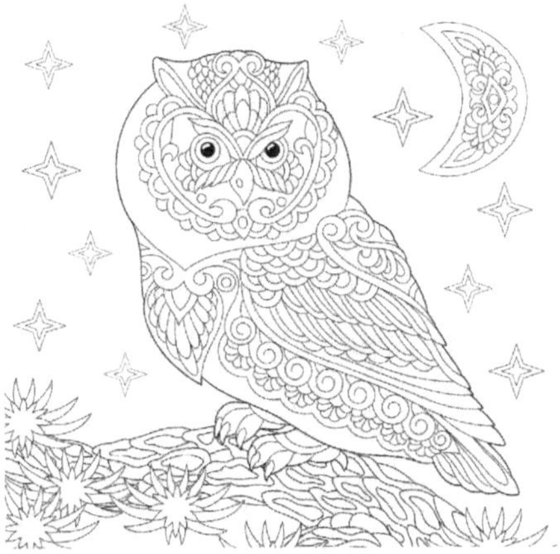

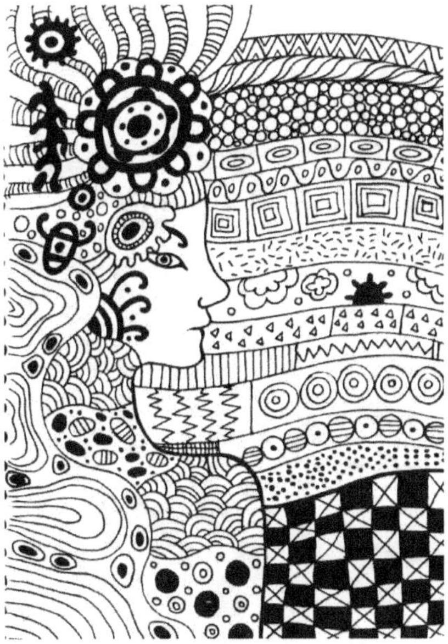

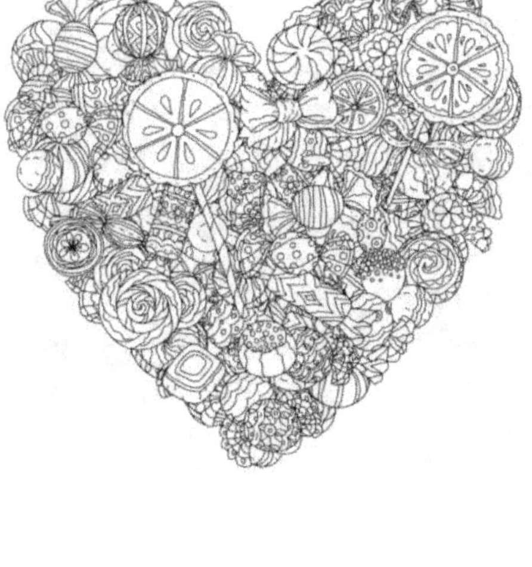

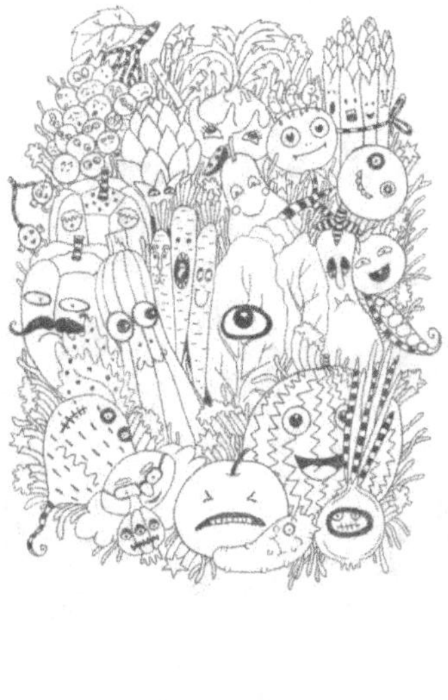

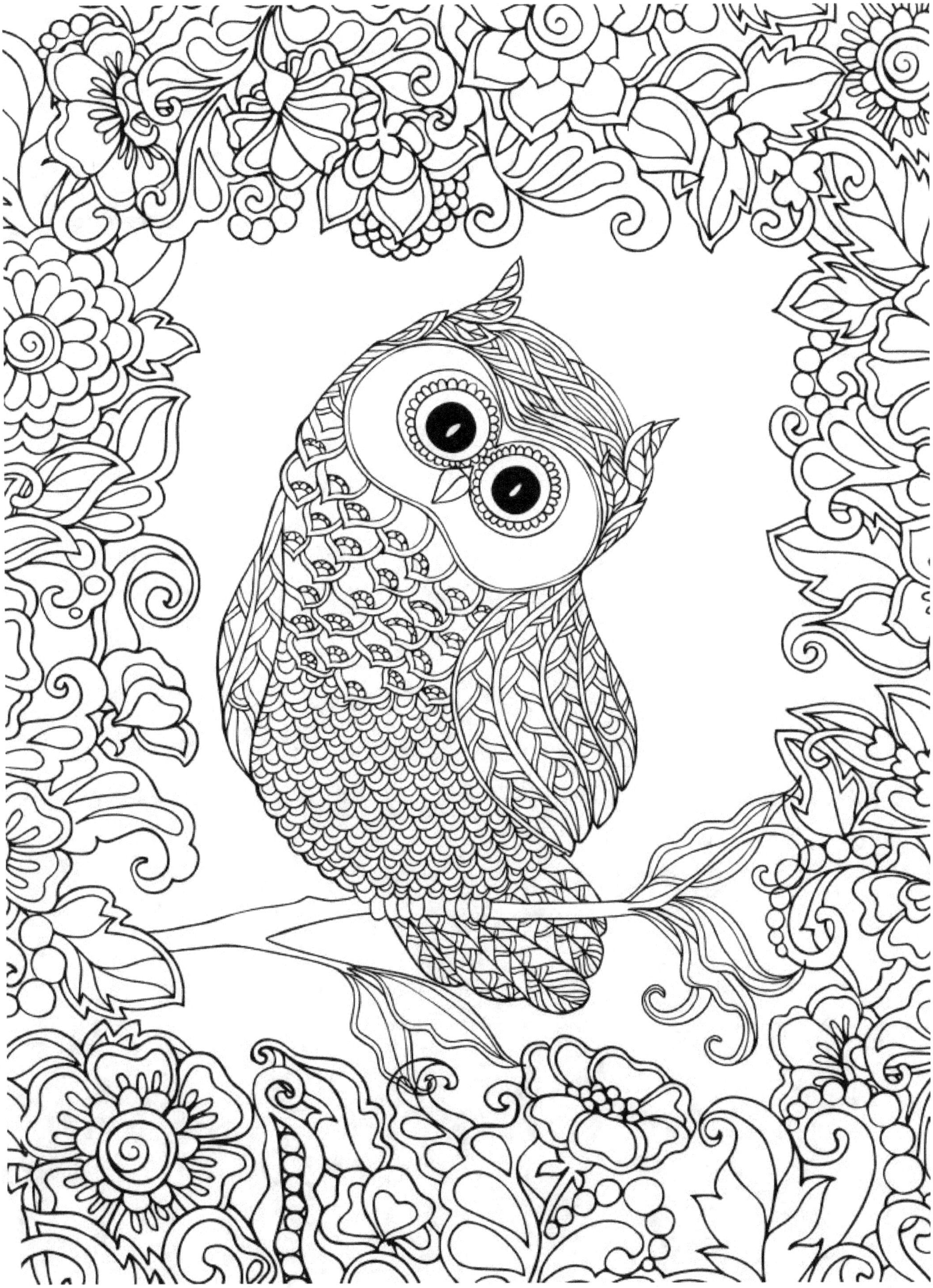

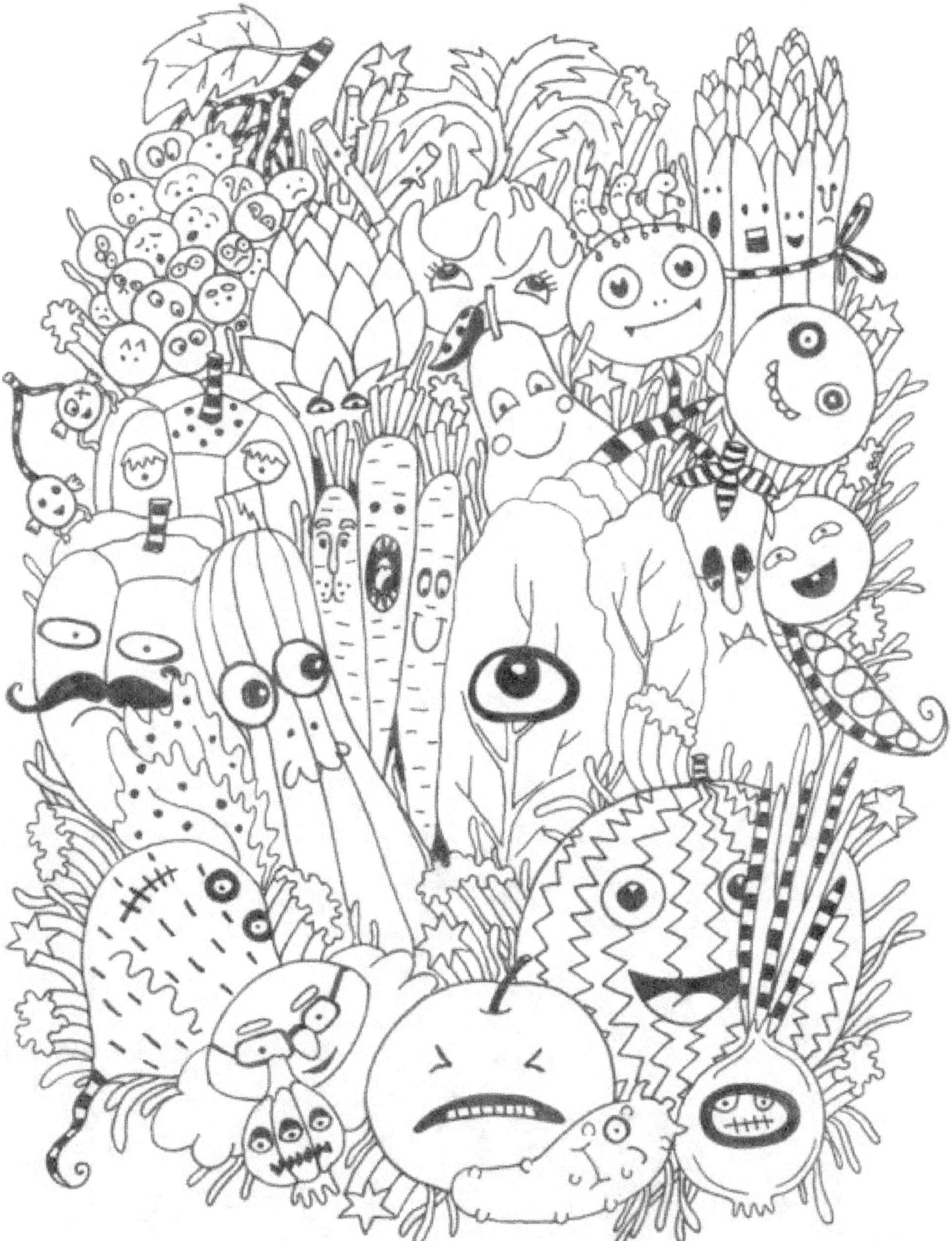

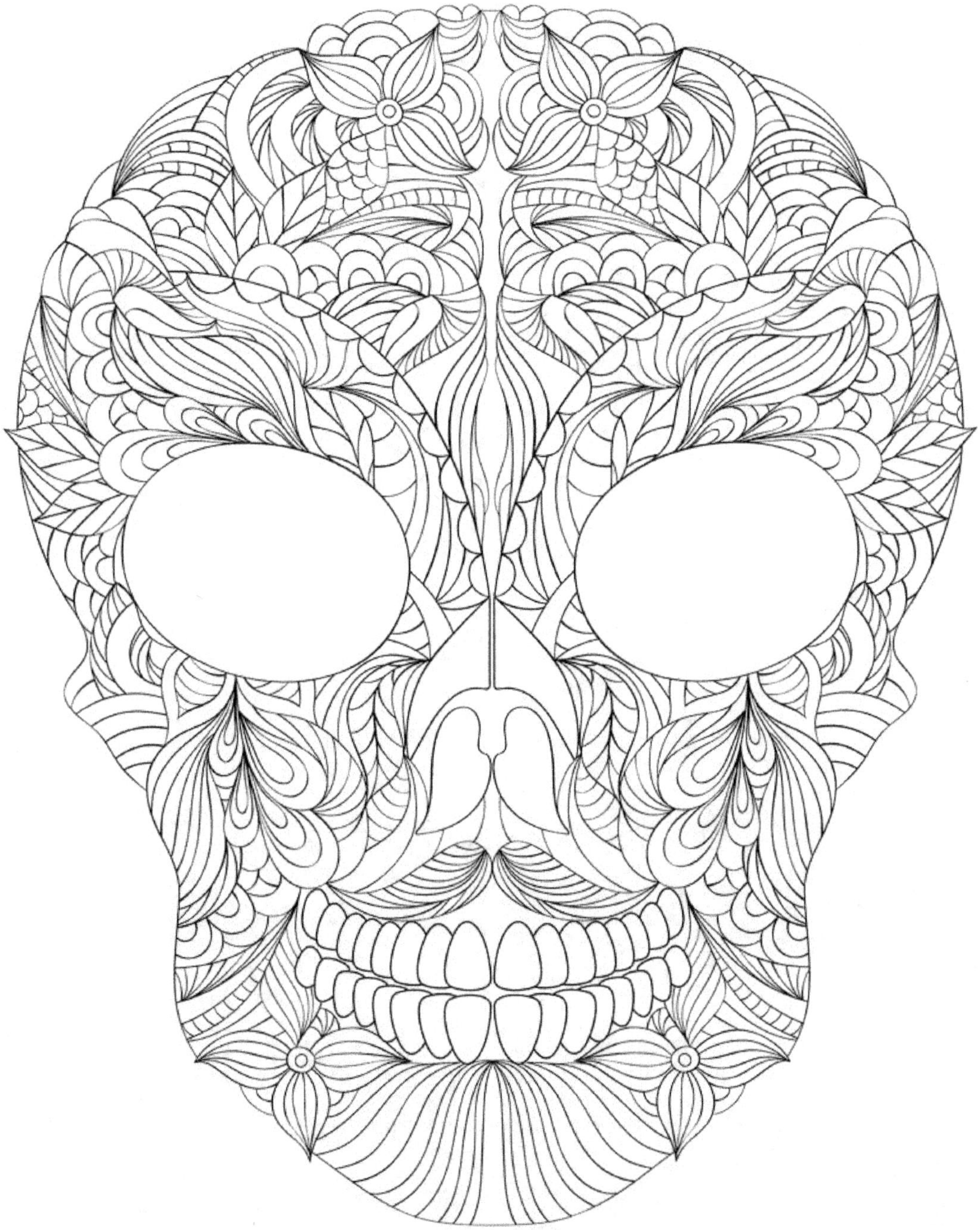

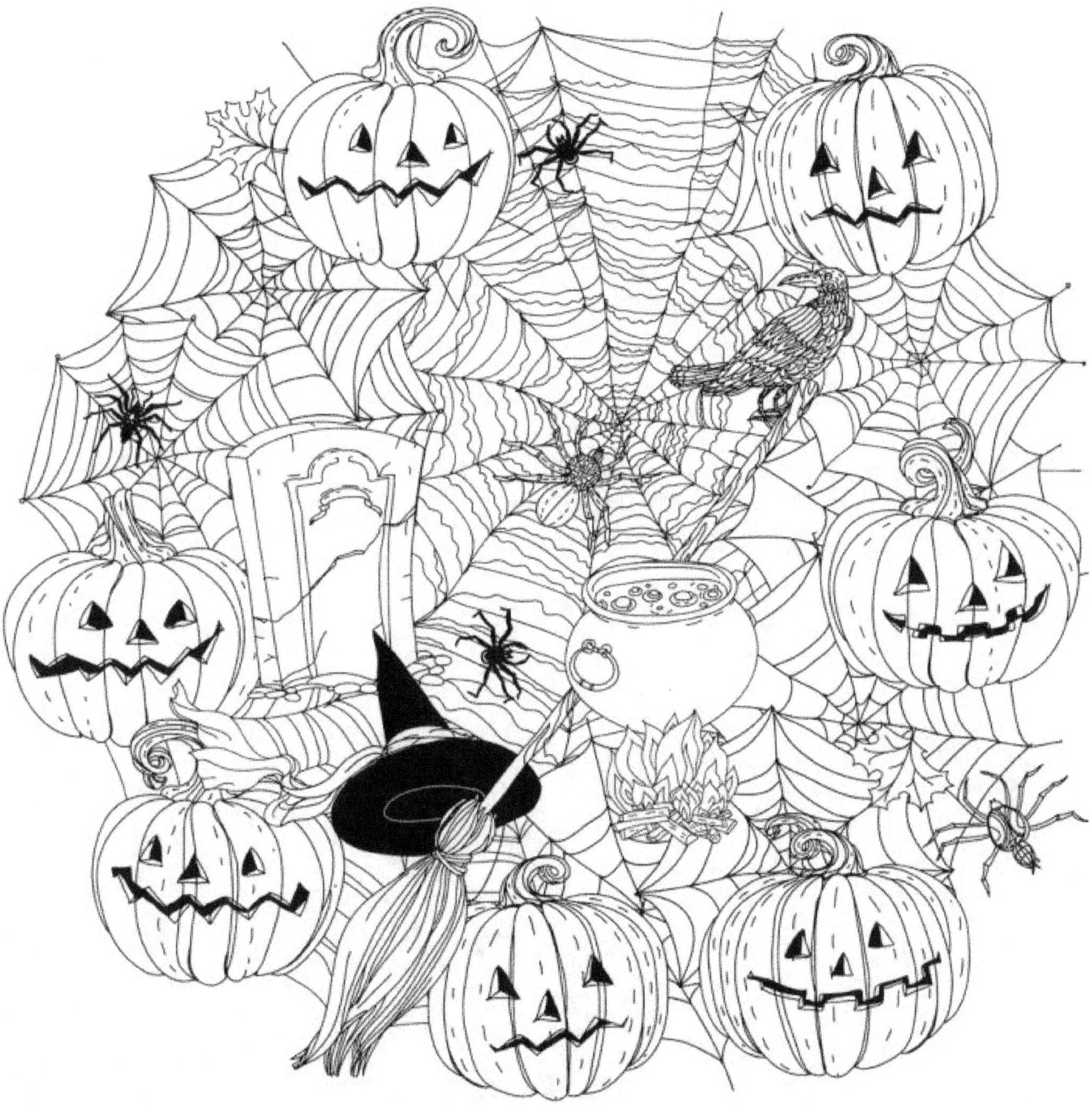

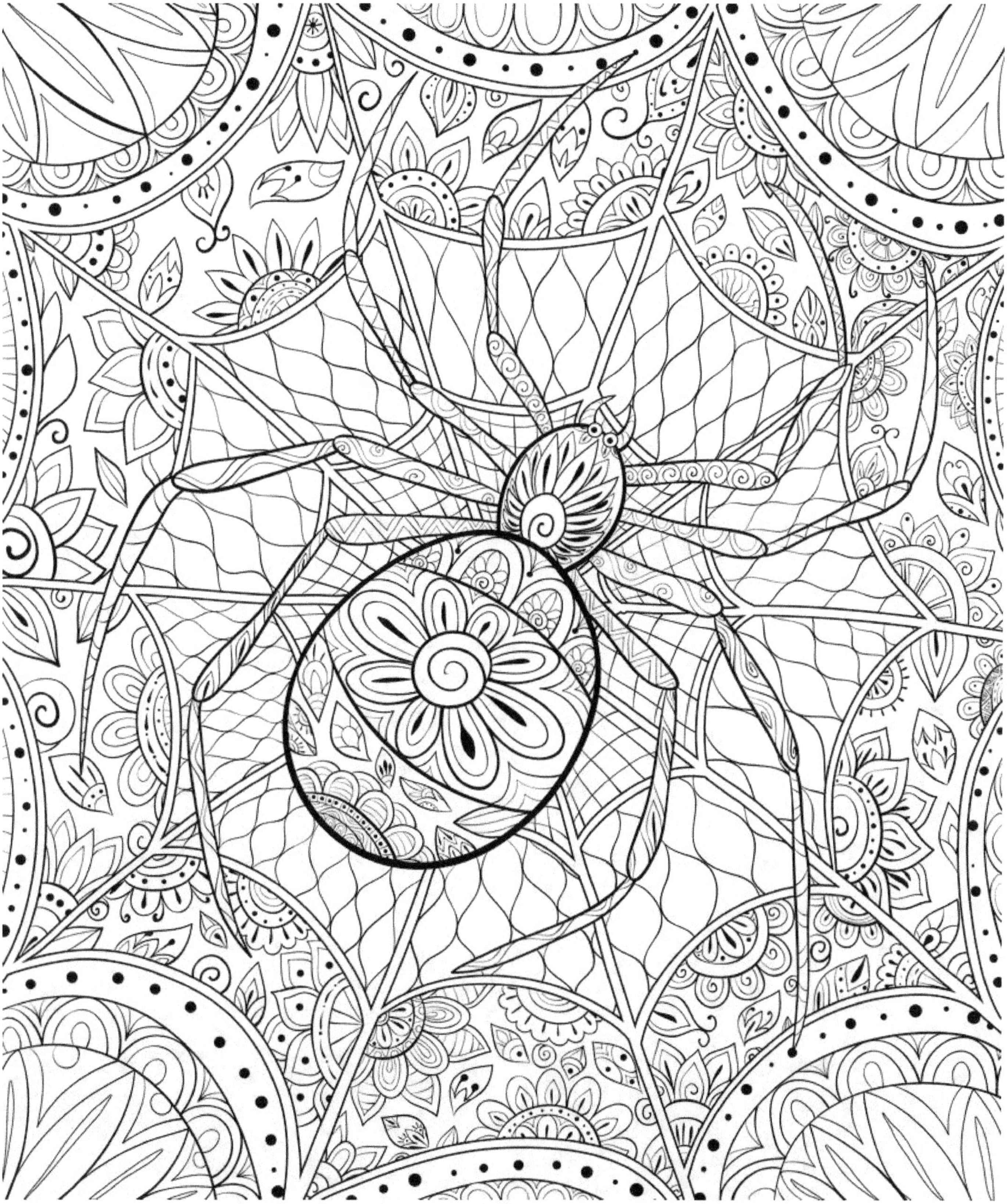

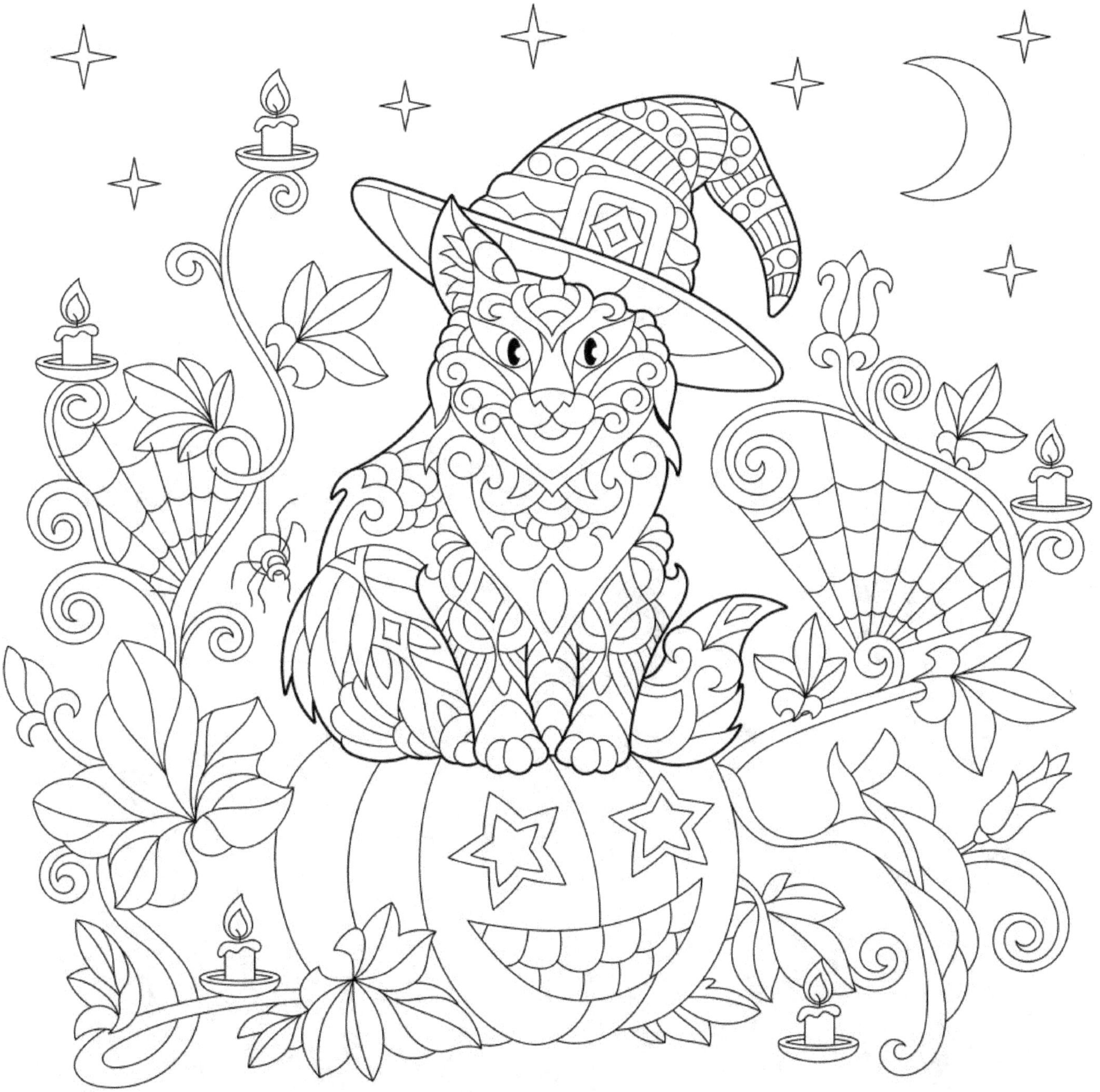

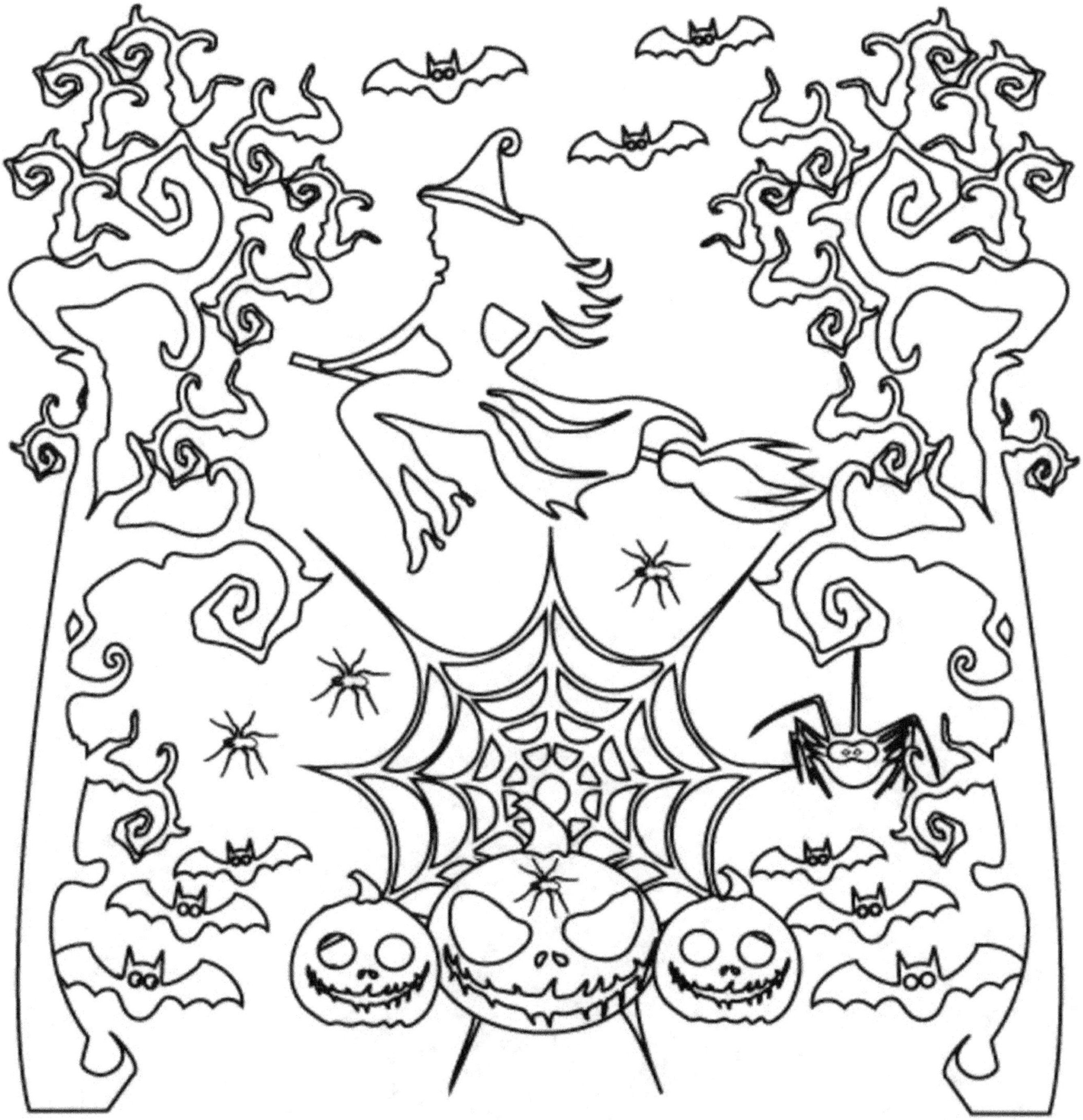

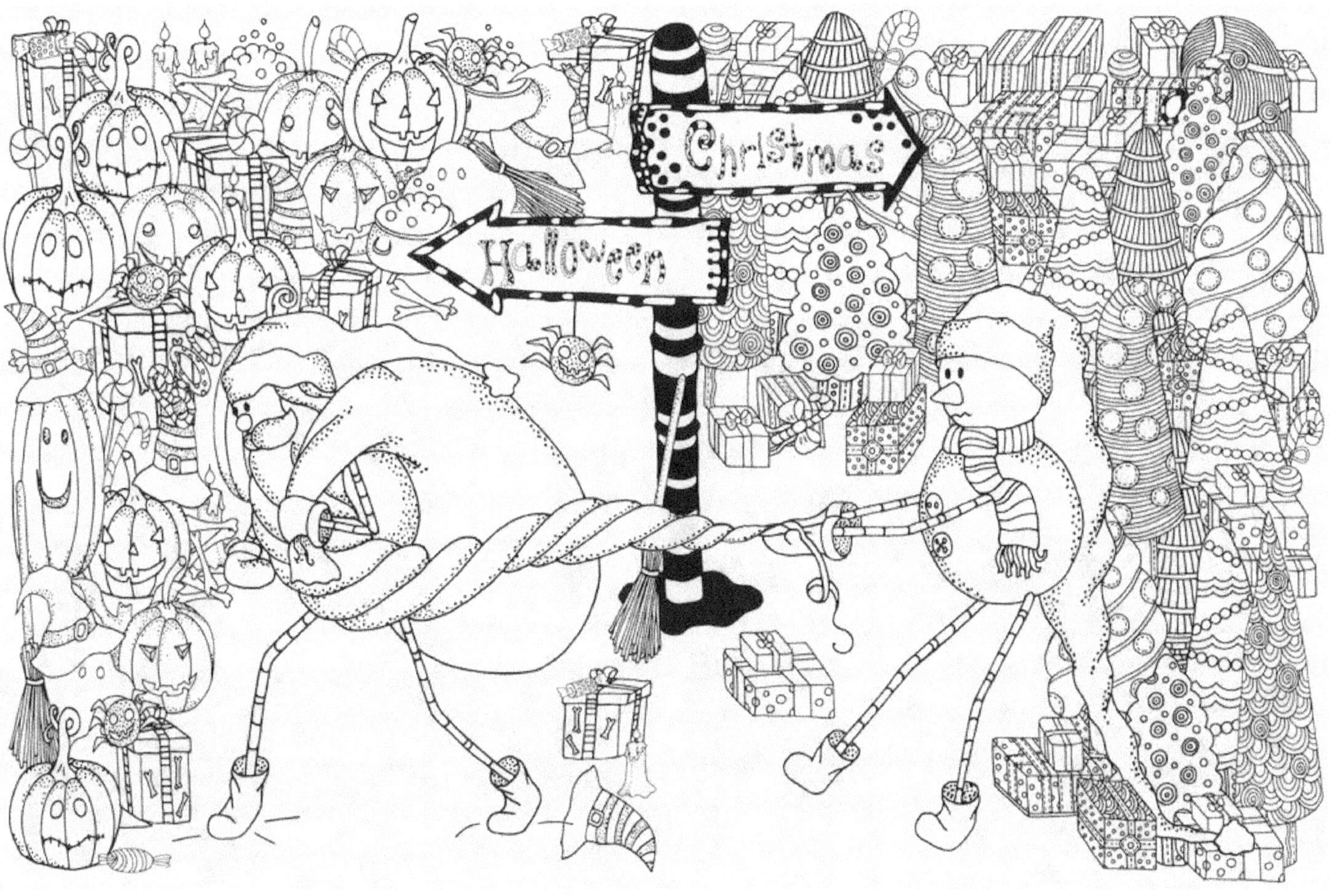
Christmas
Halloween

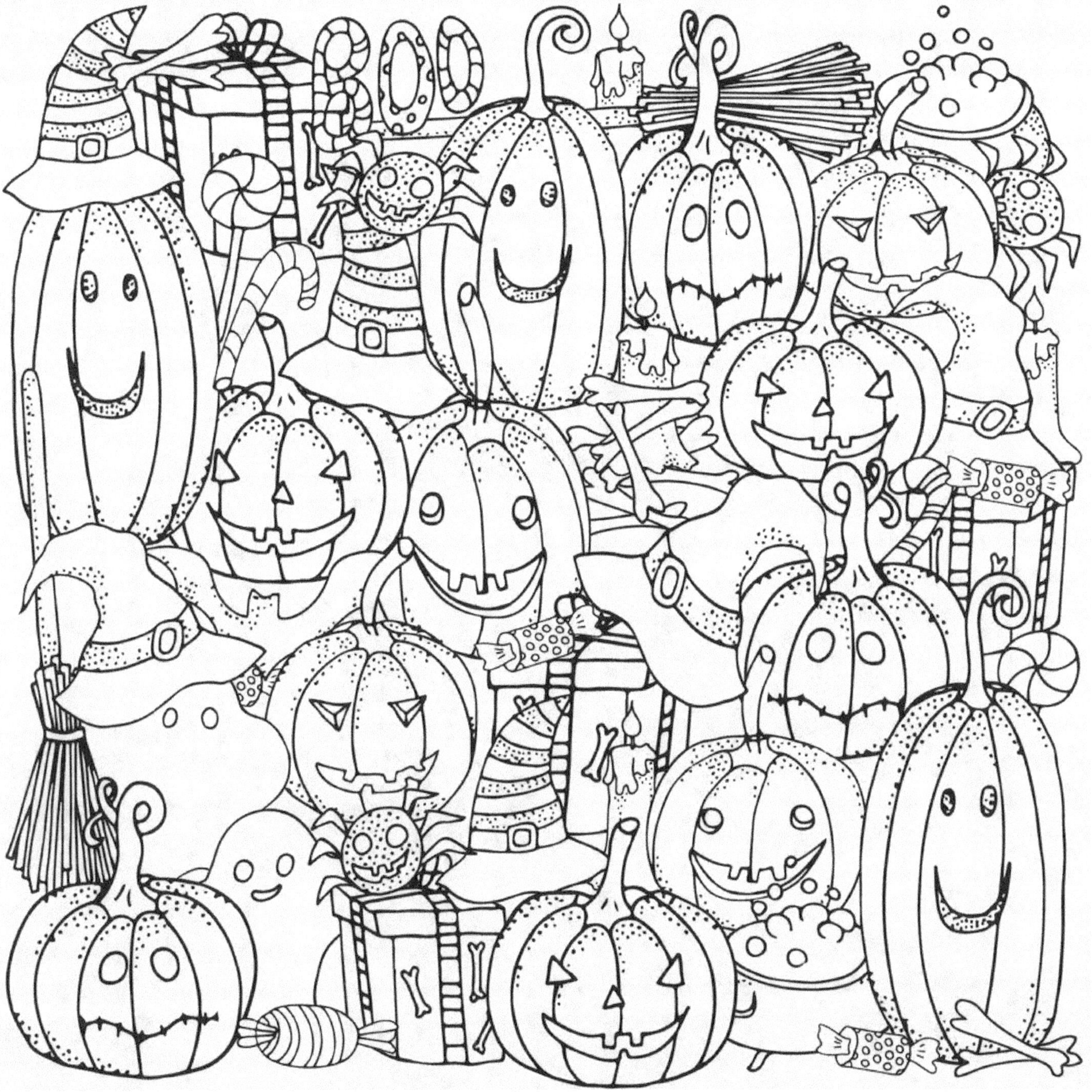
BOO

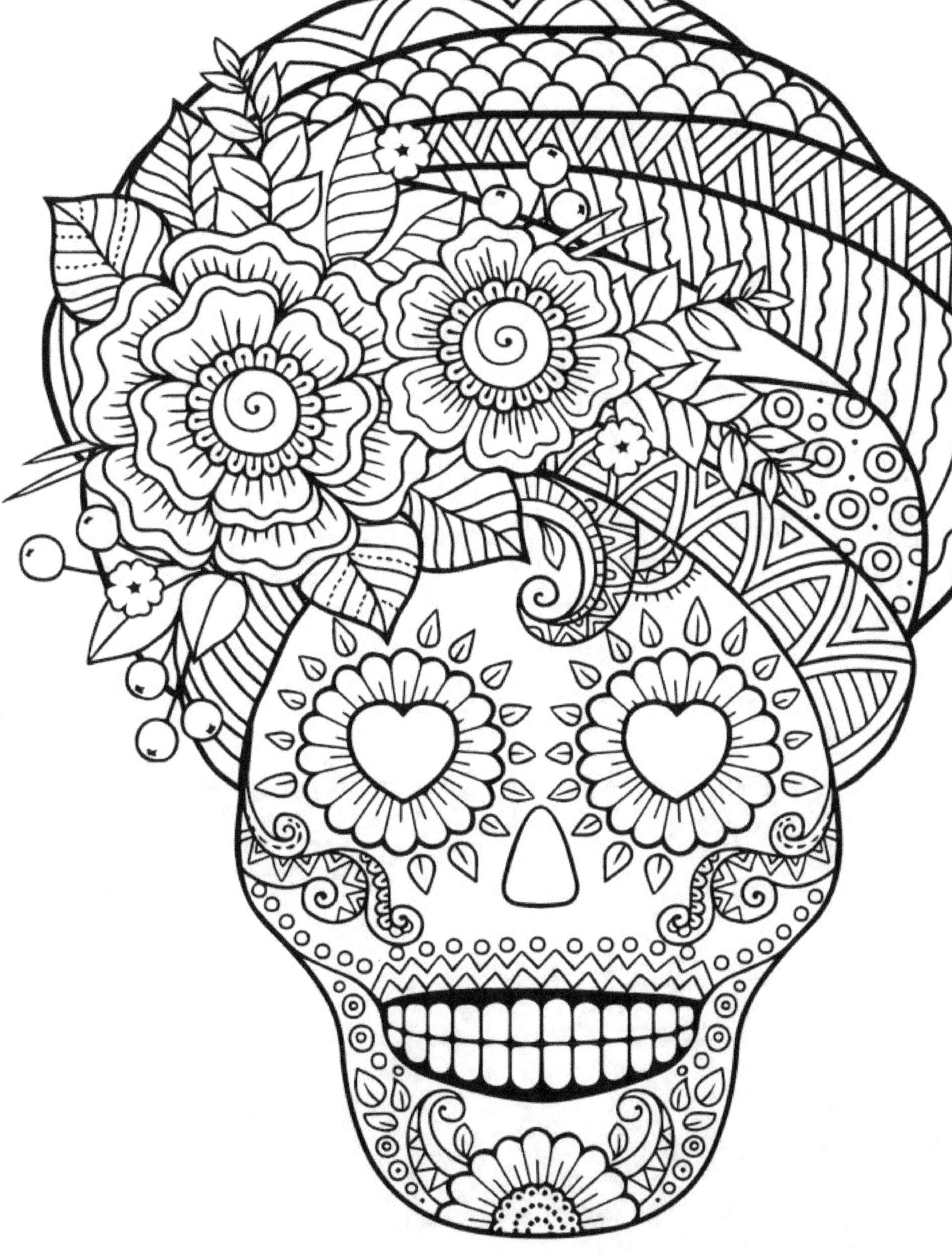

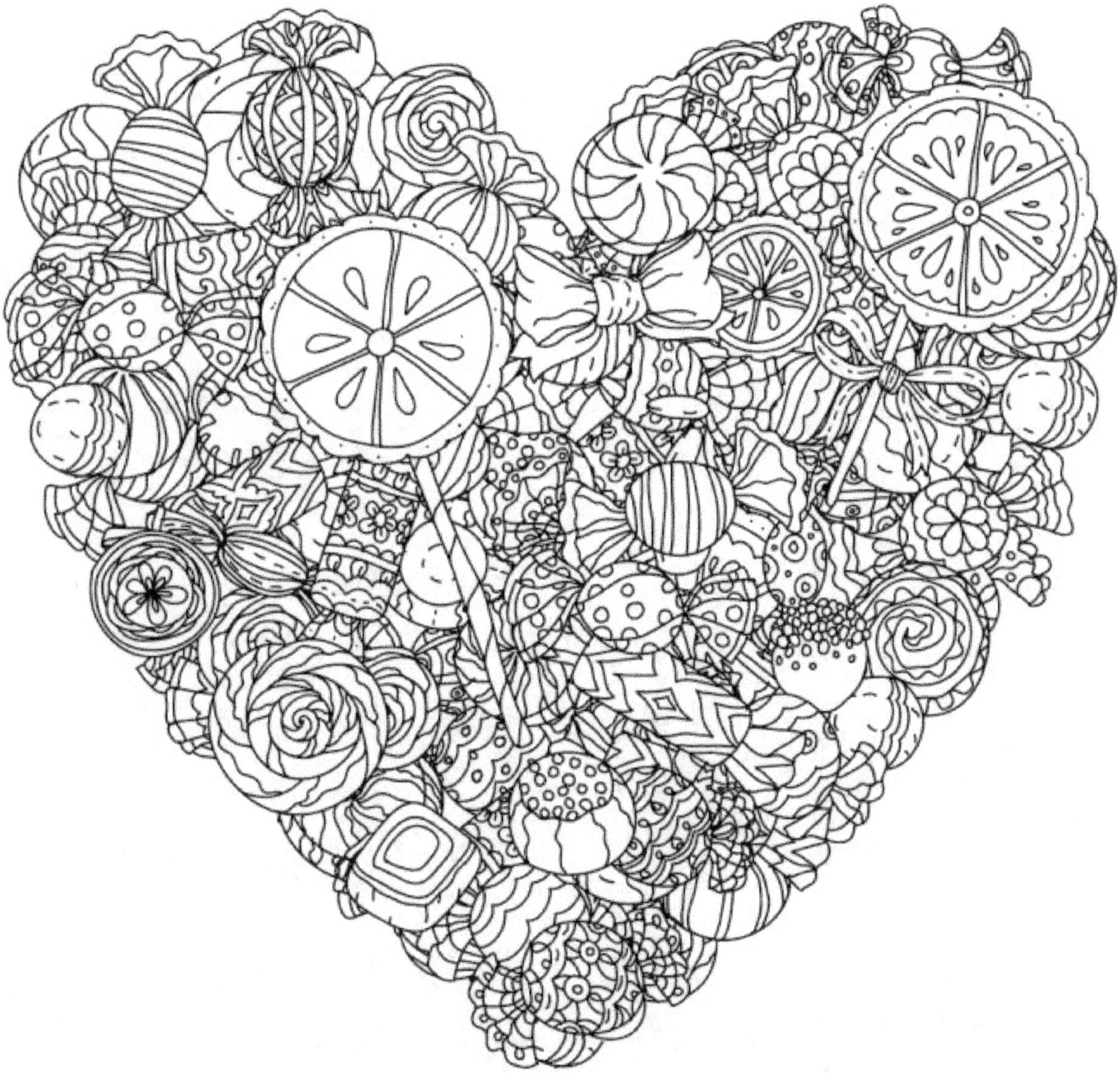

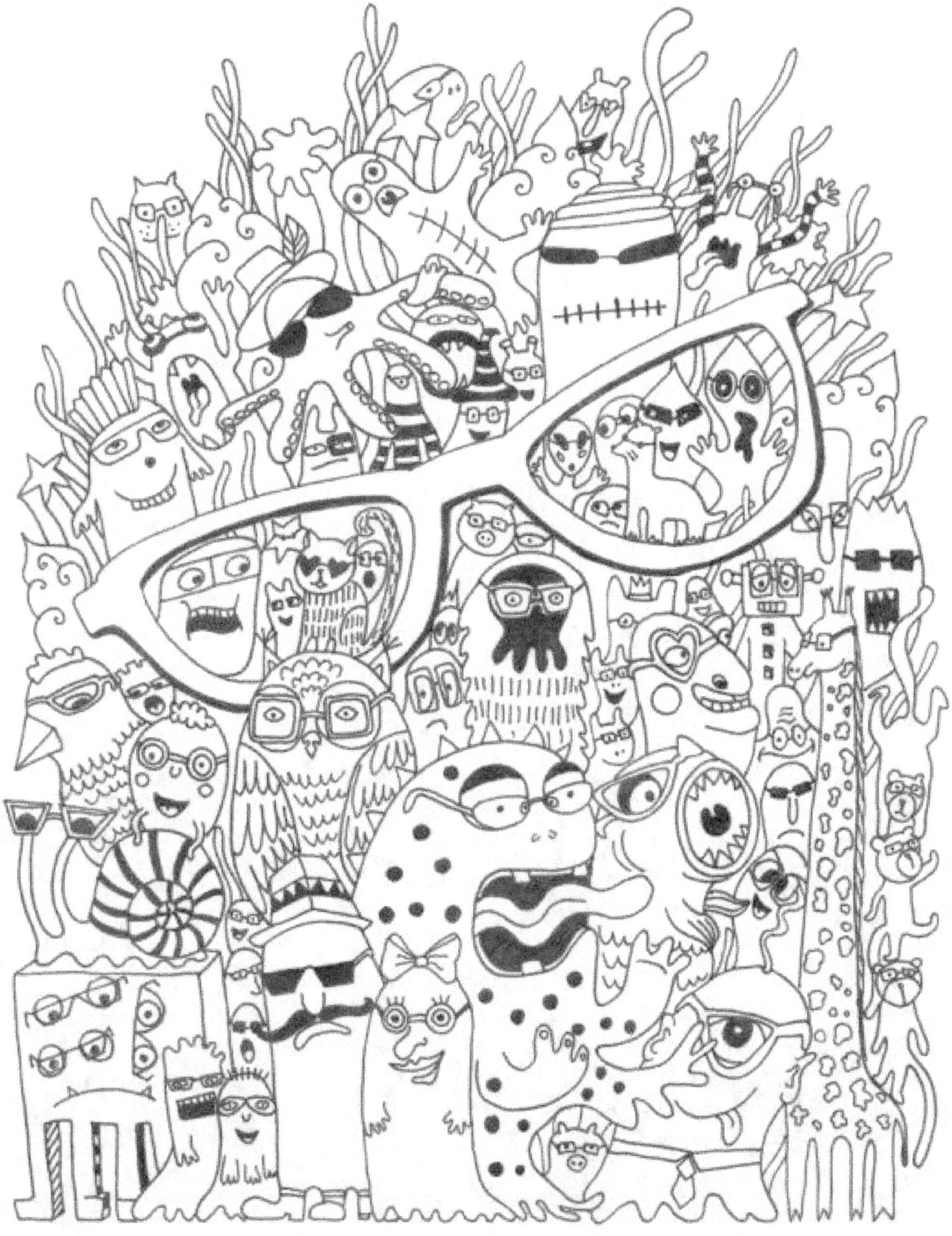

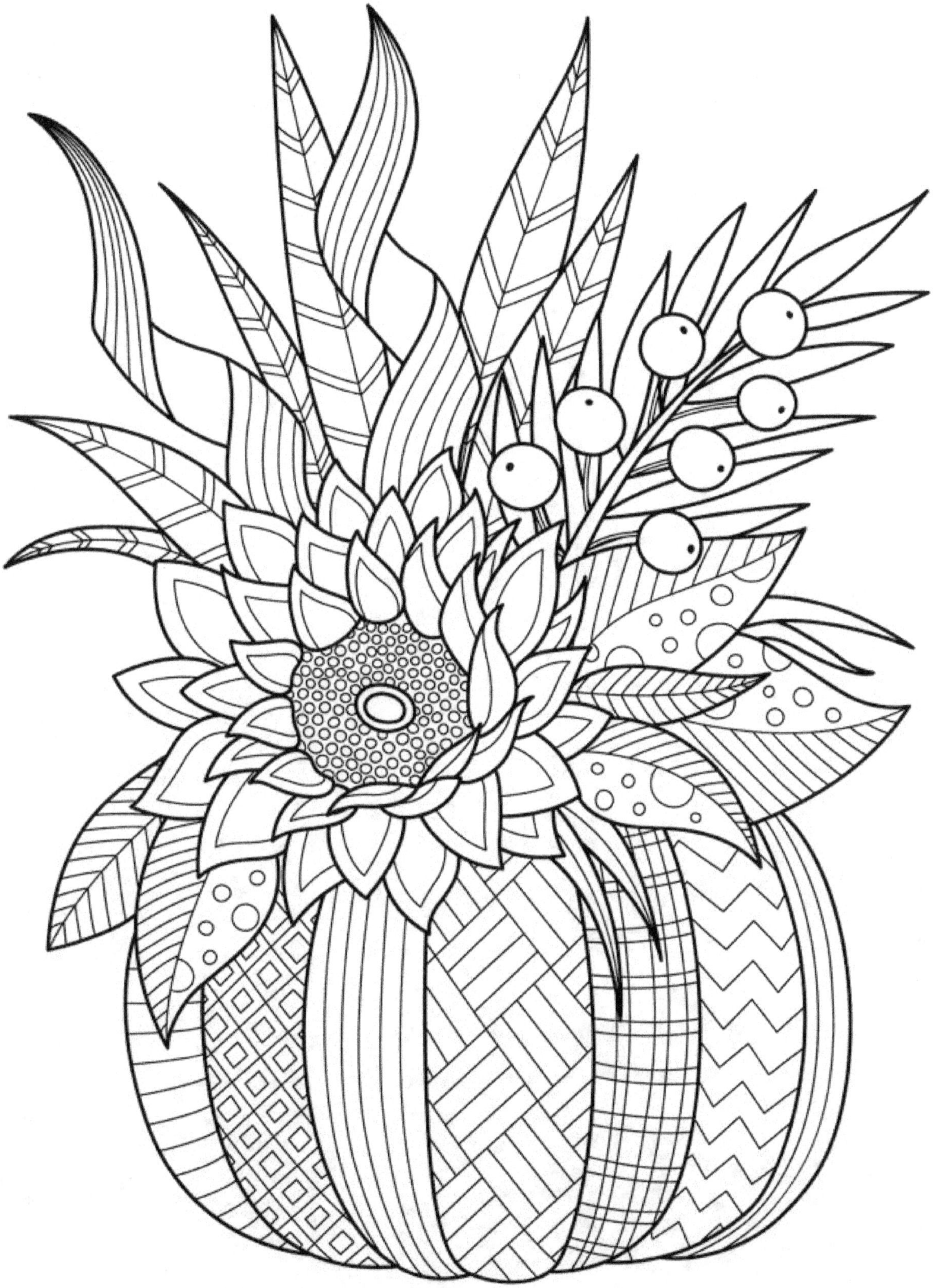

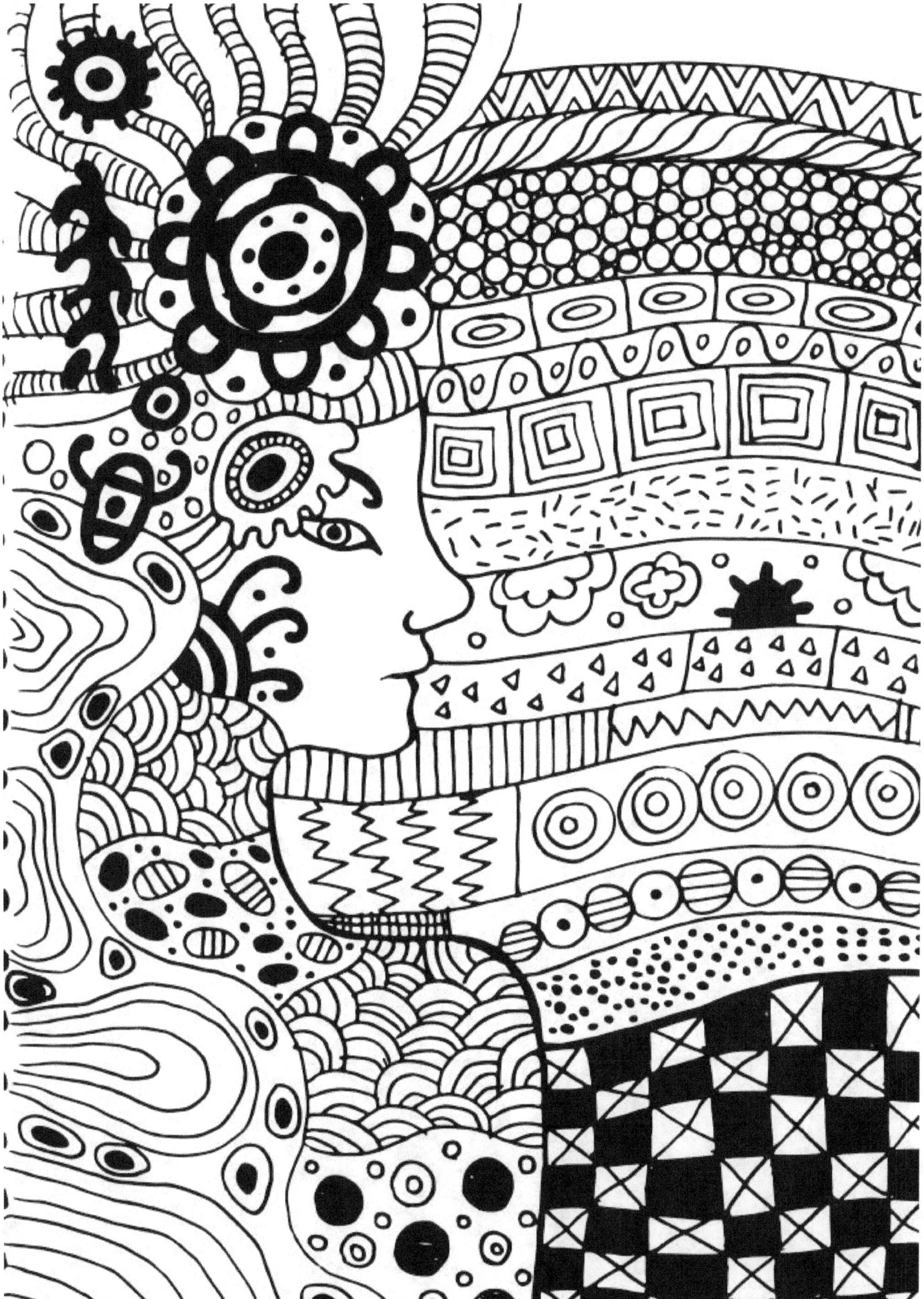

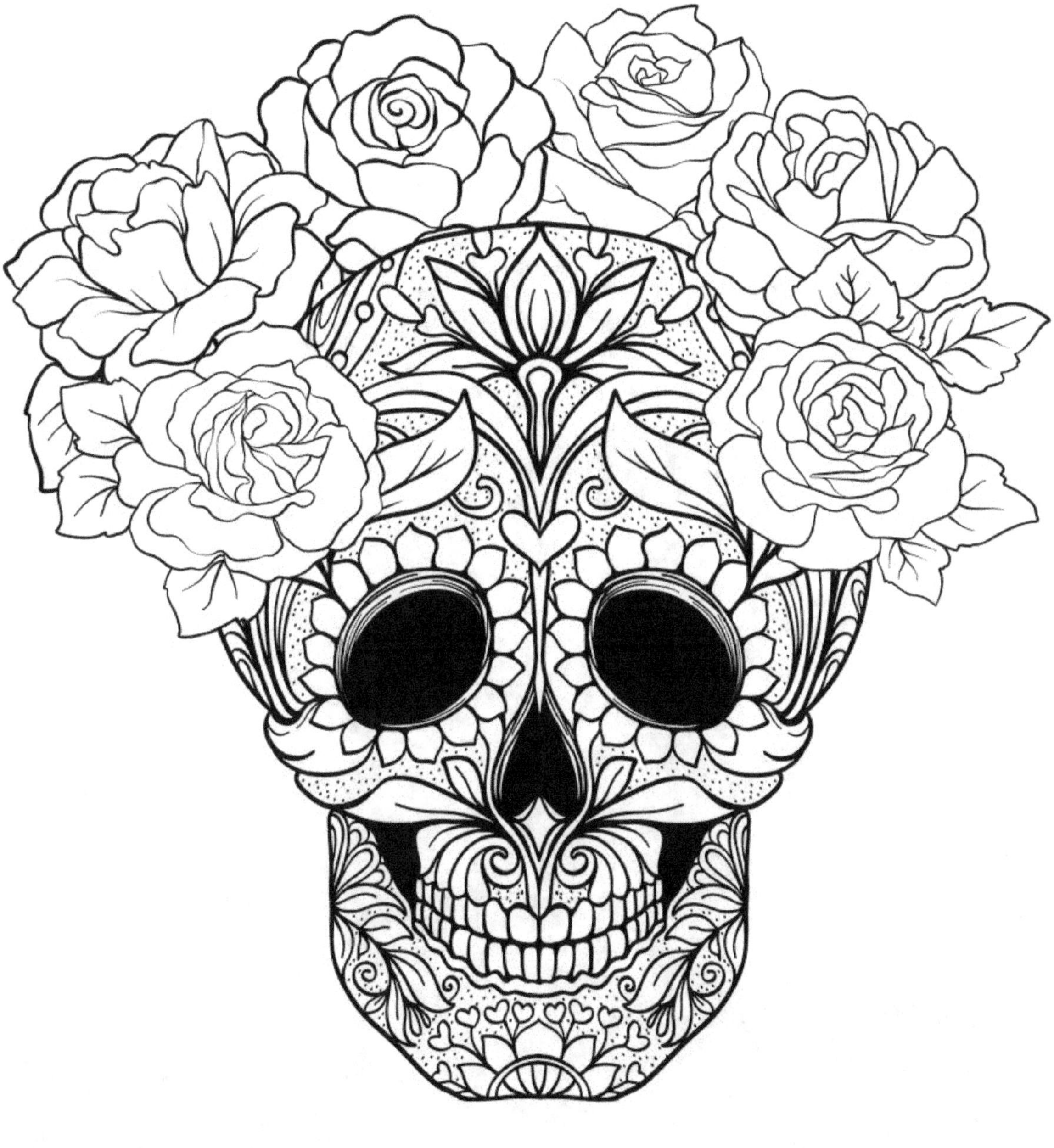

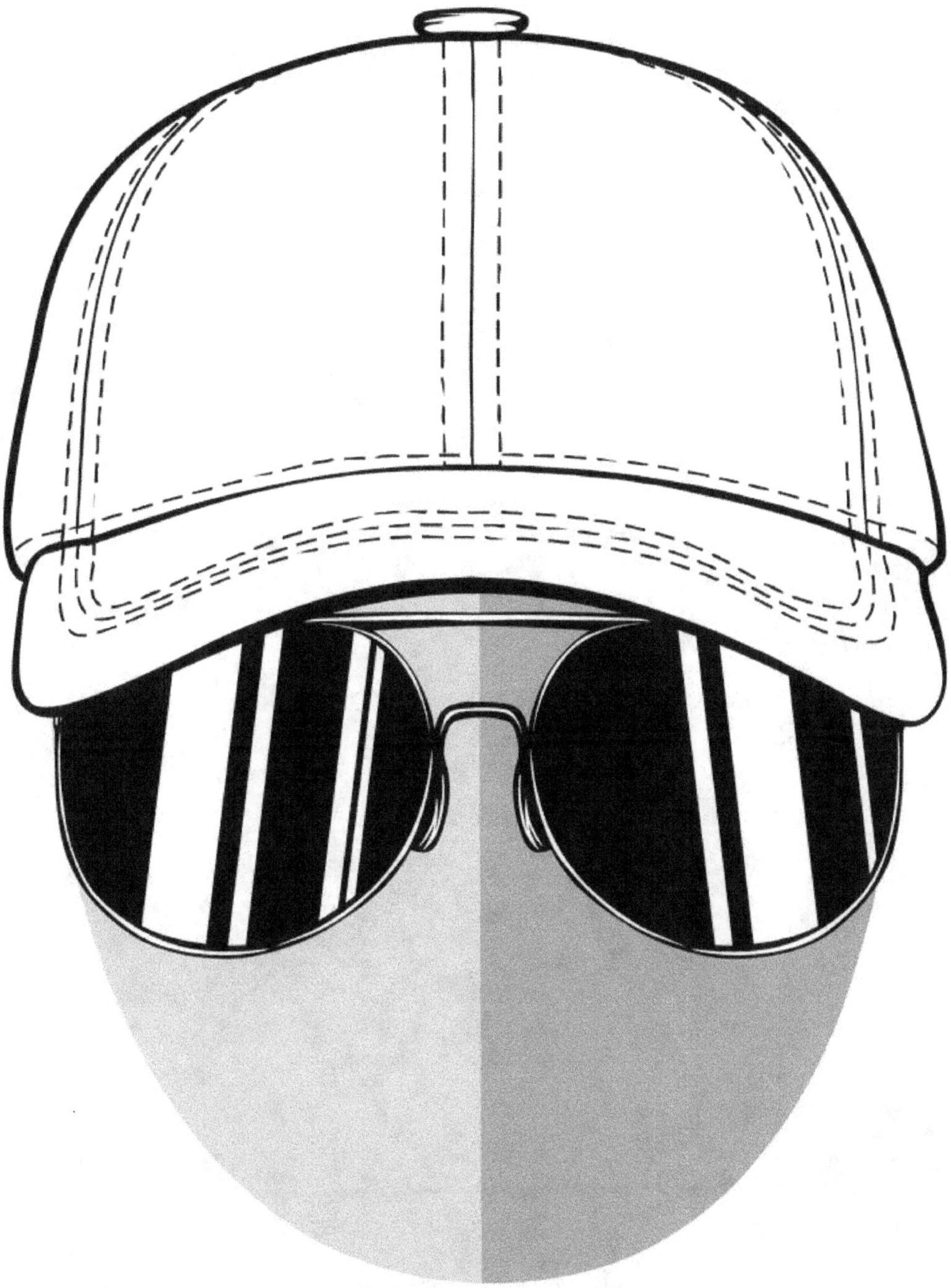

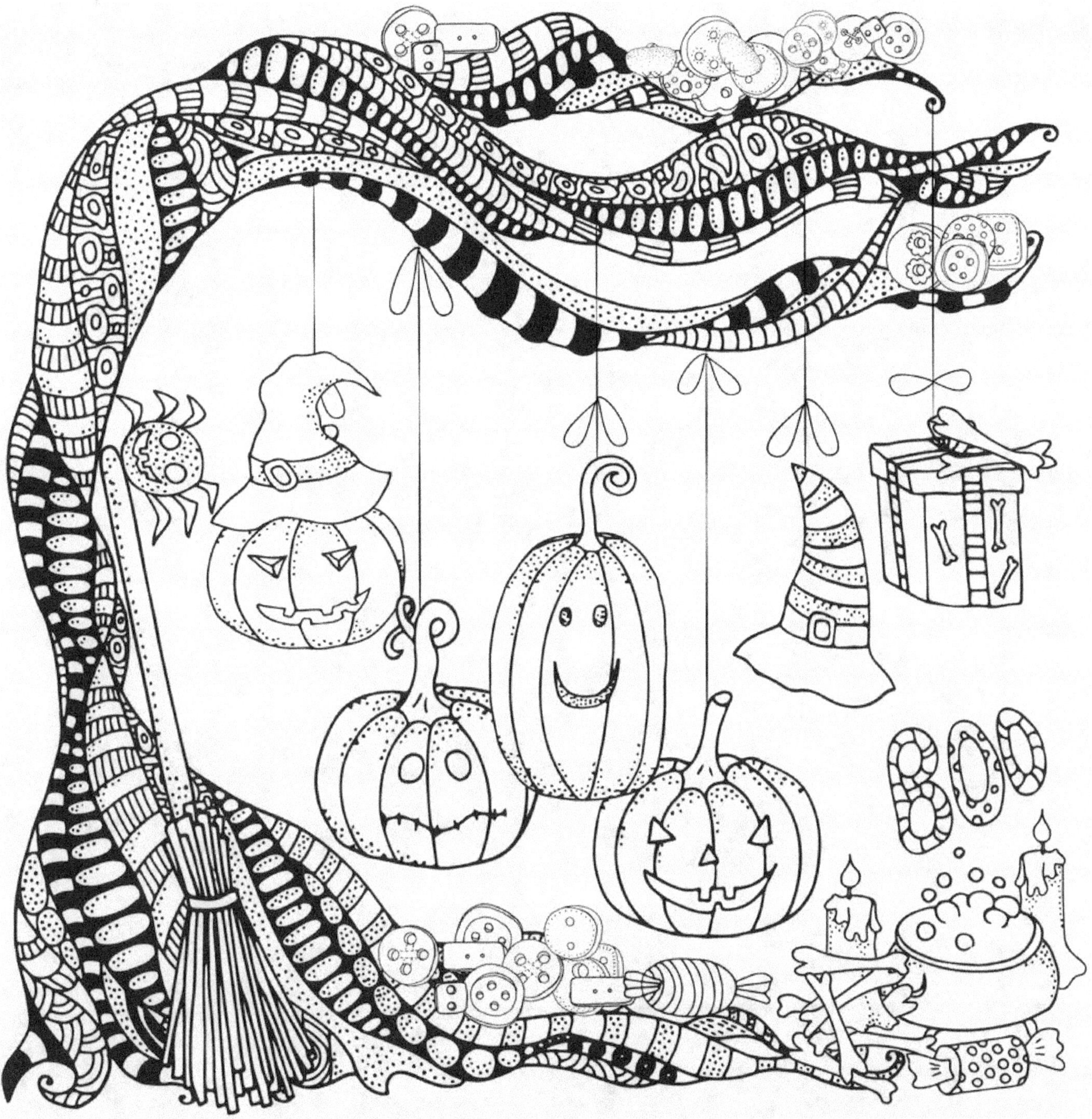
BOO

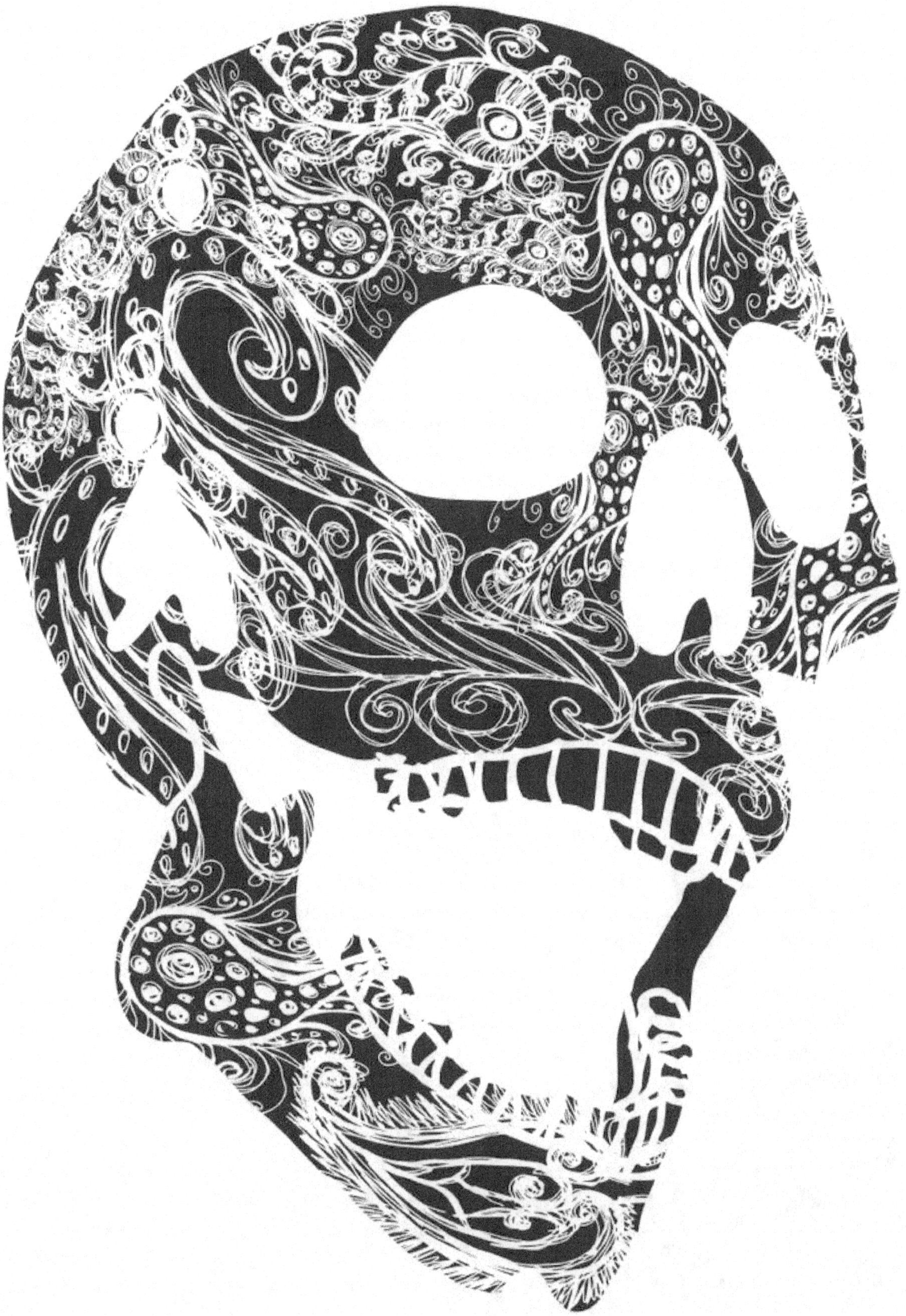

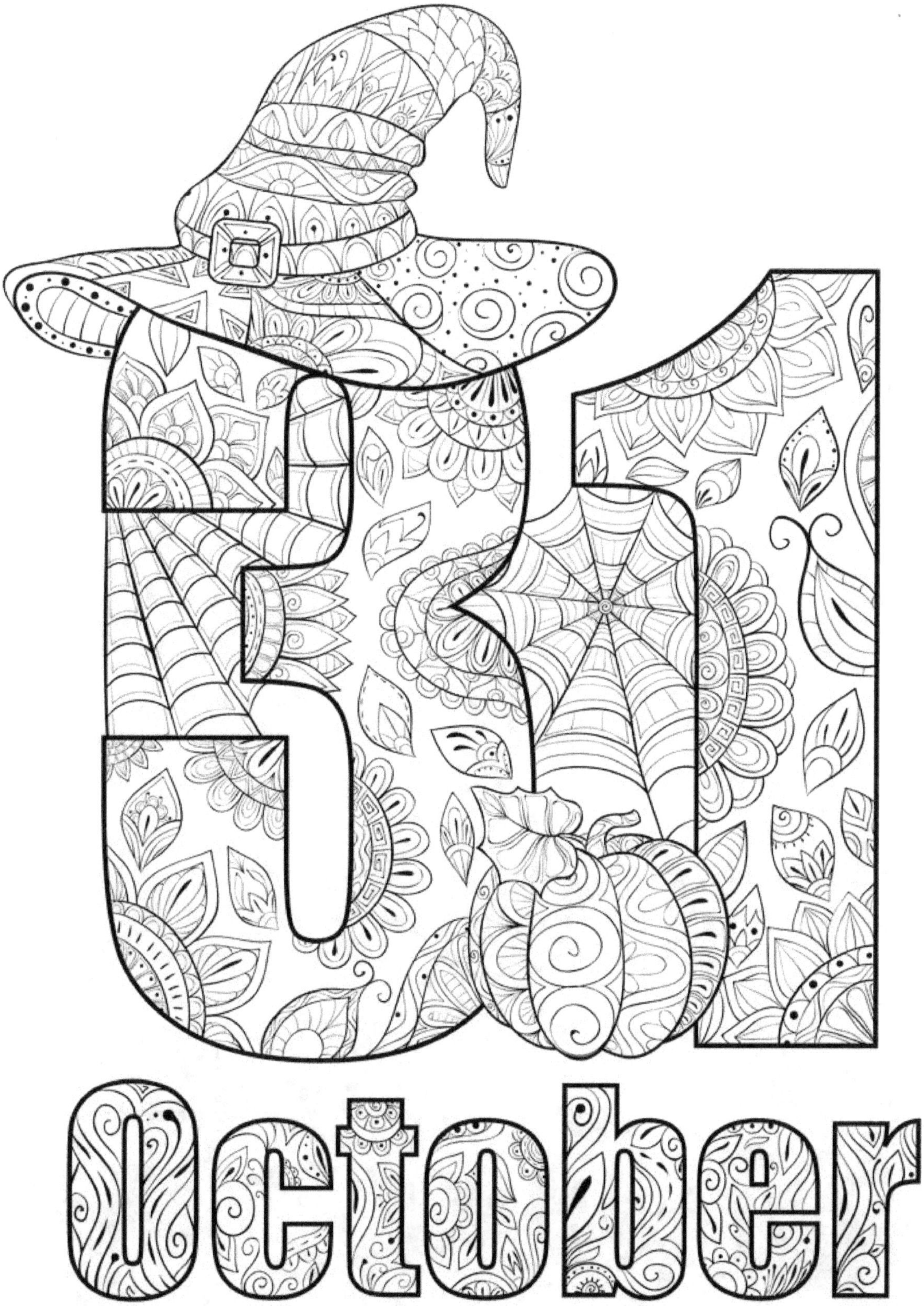
31
October

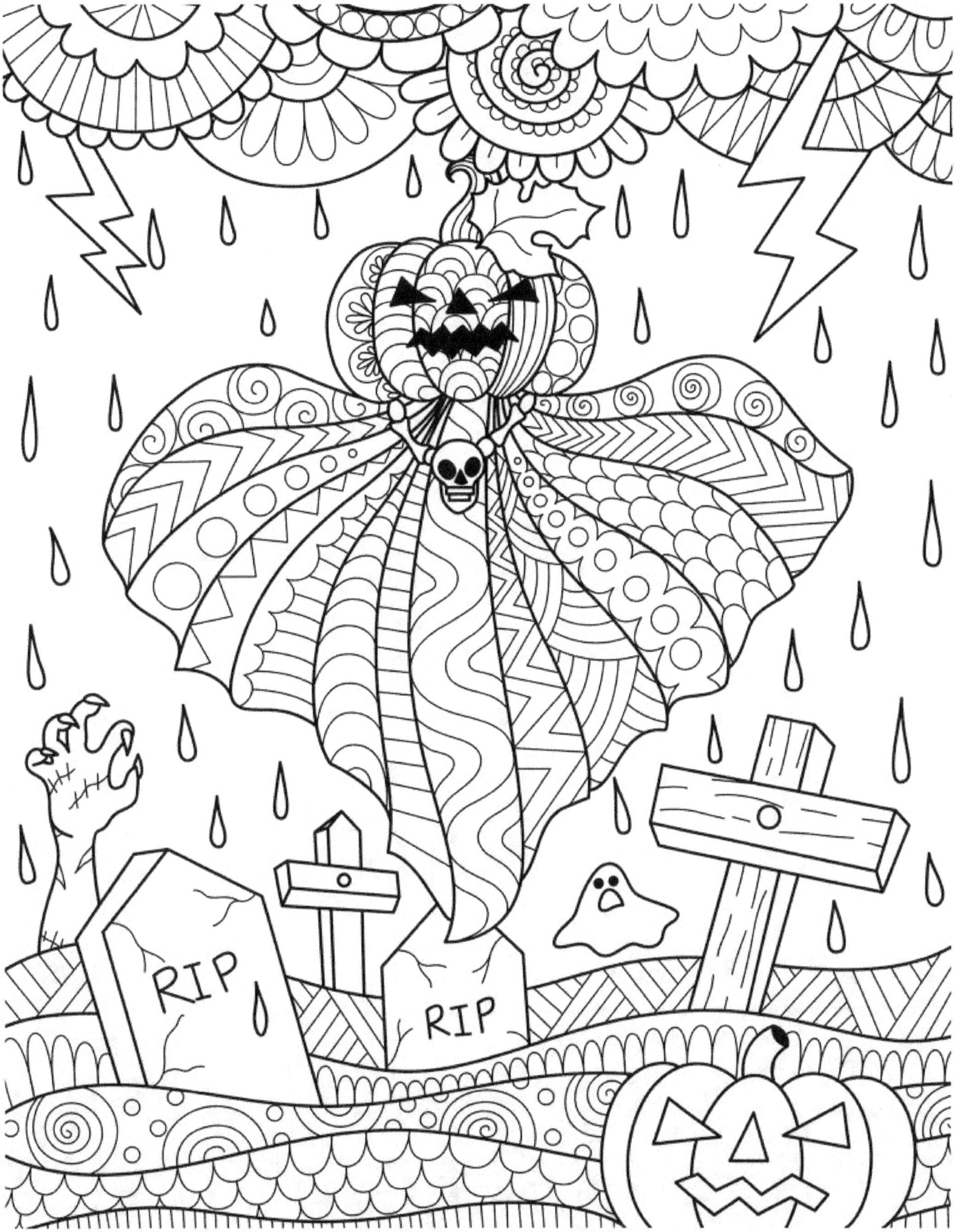
RIP
RIP

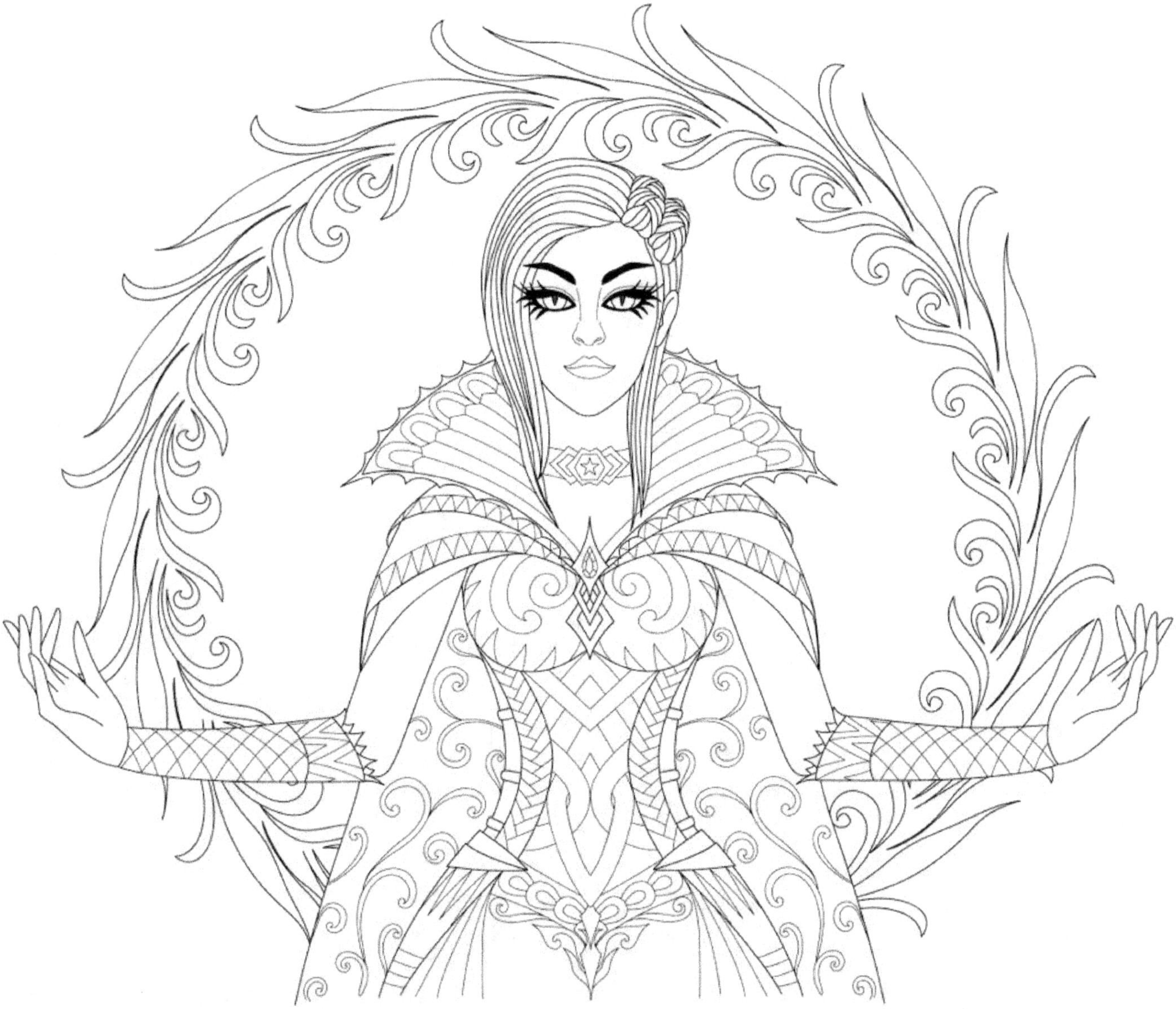

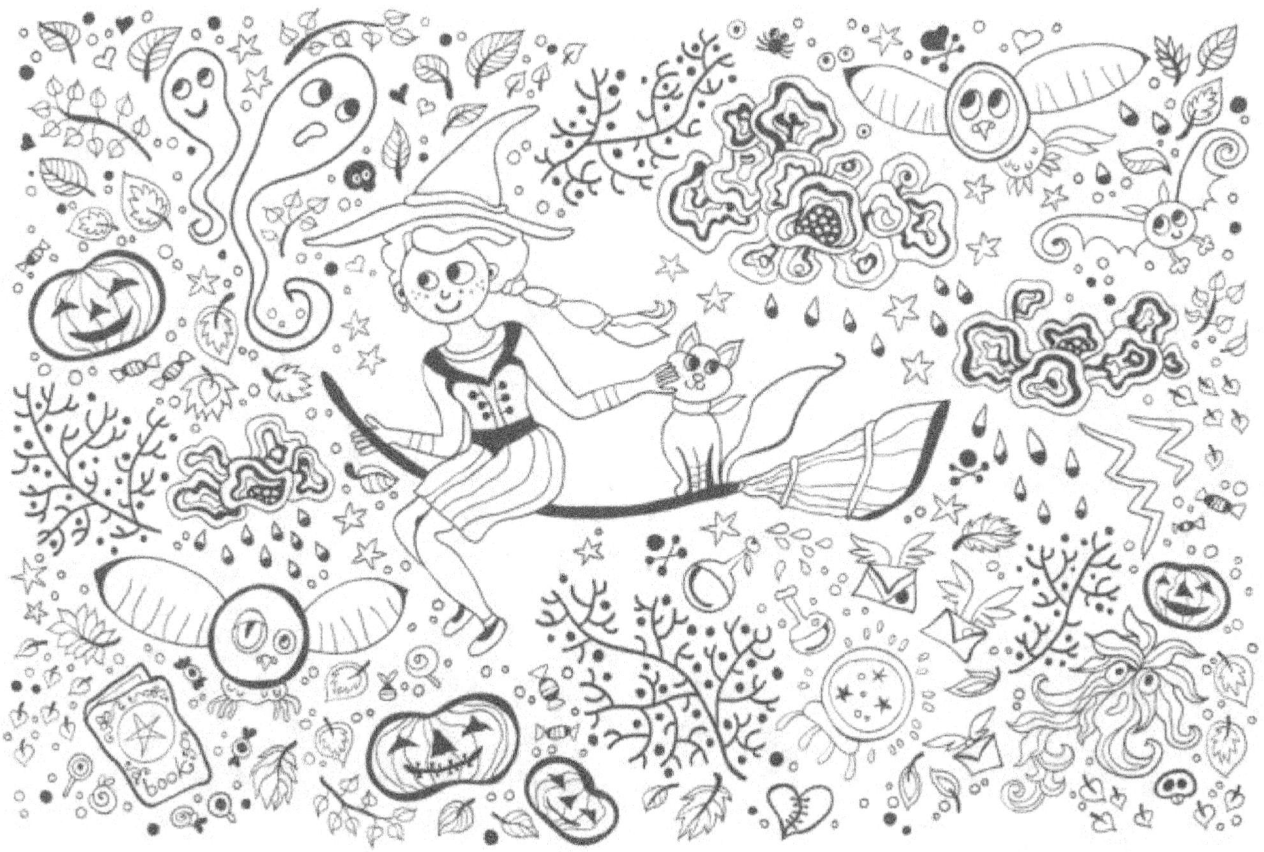

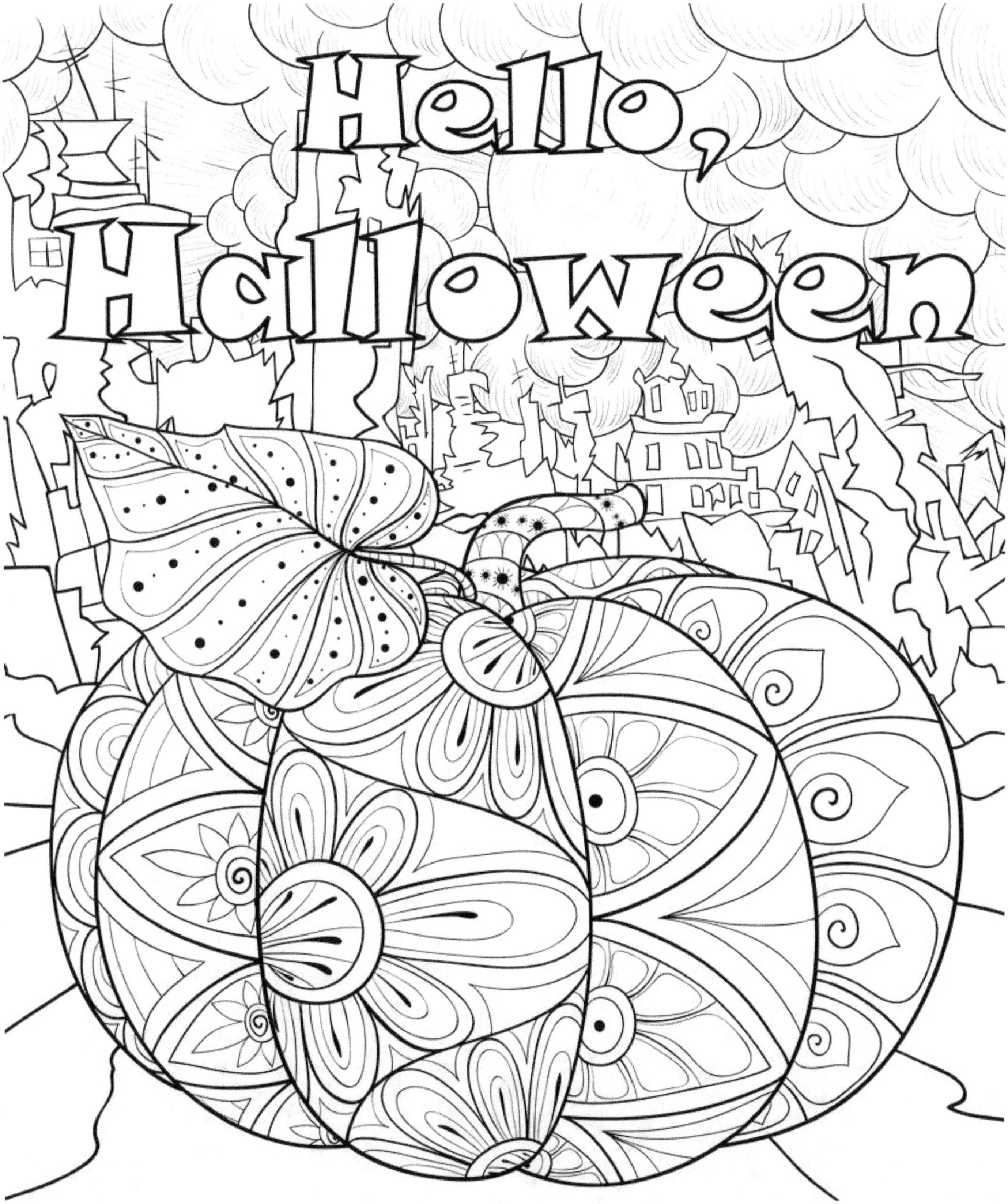
Hello, Halloween

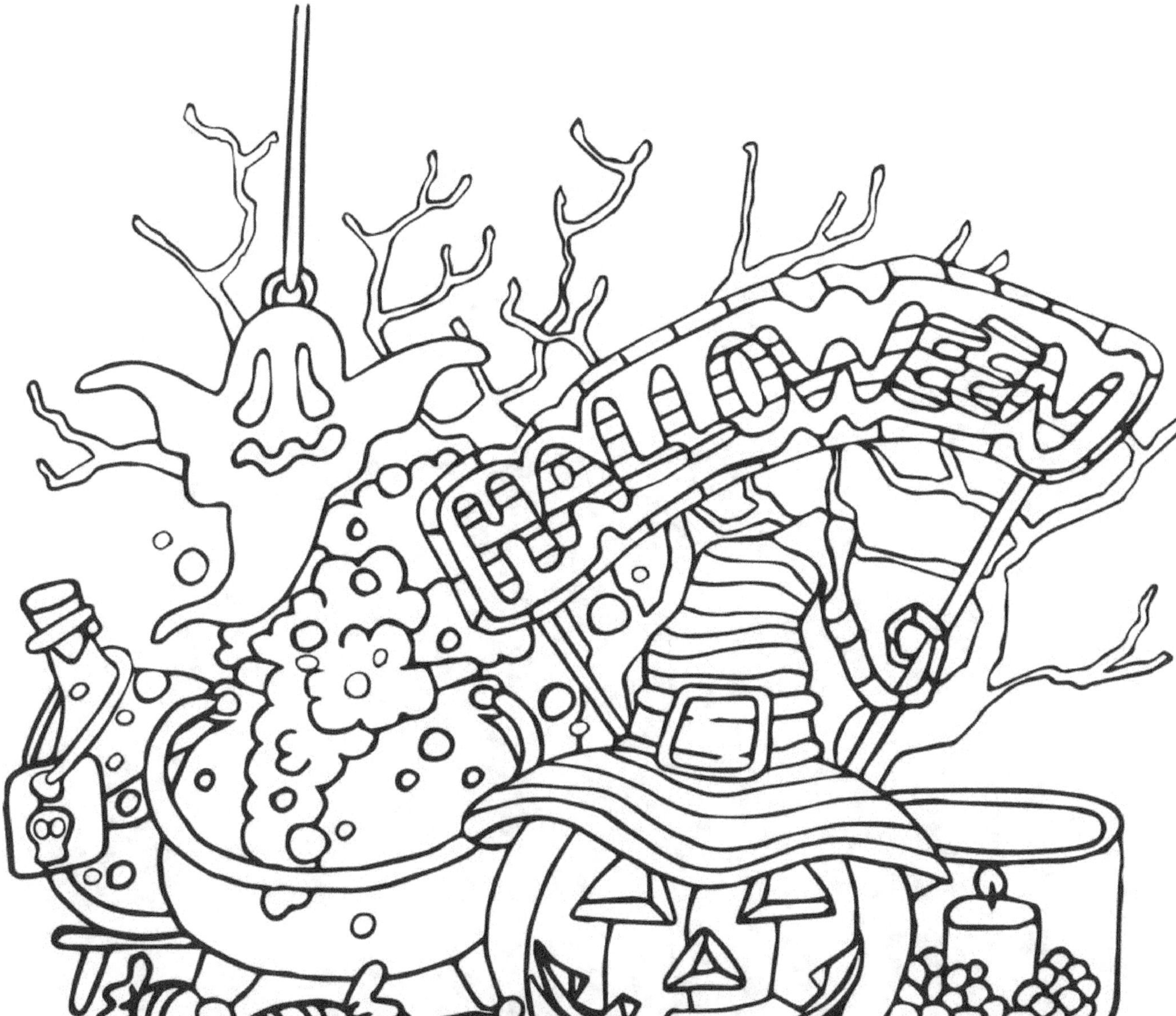
HALLOWEEN

THANK YOU!

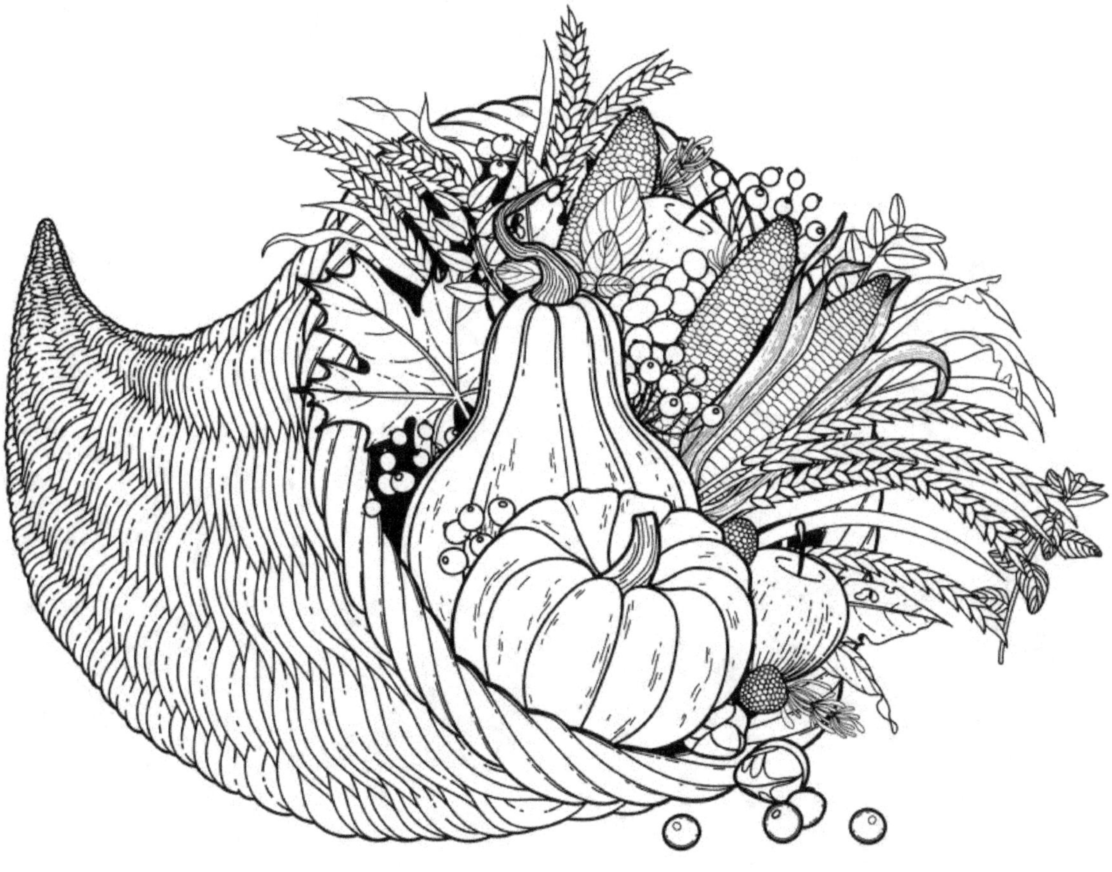

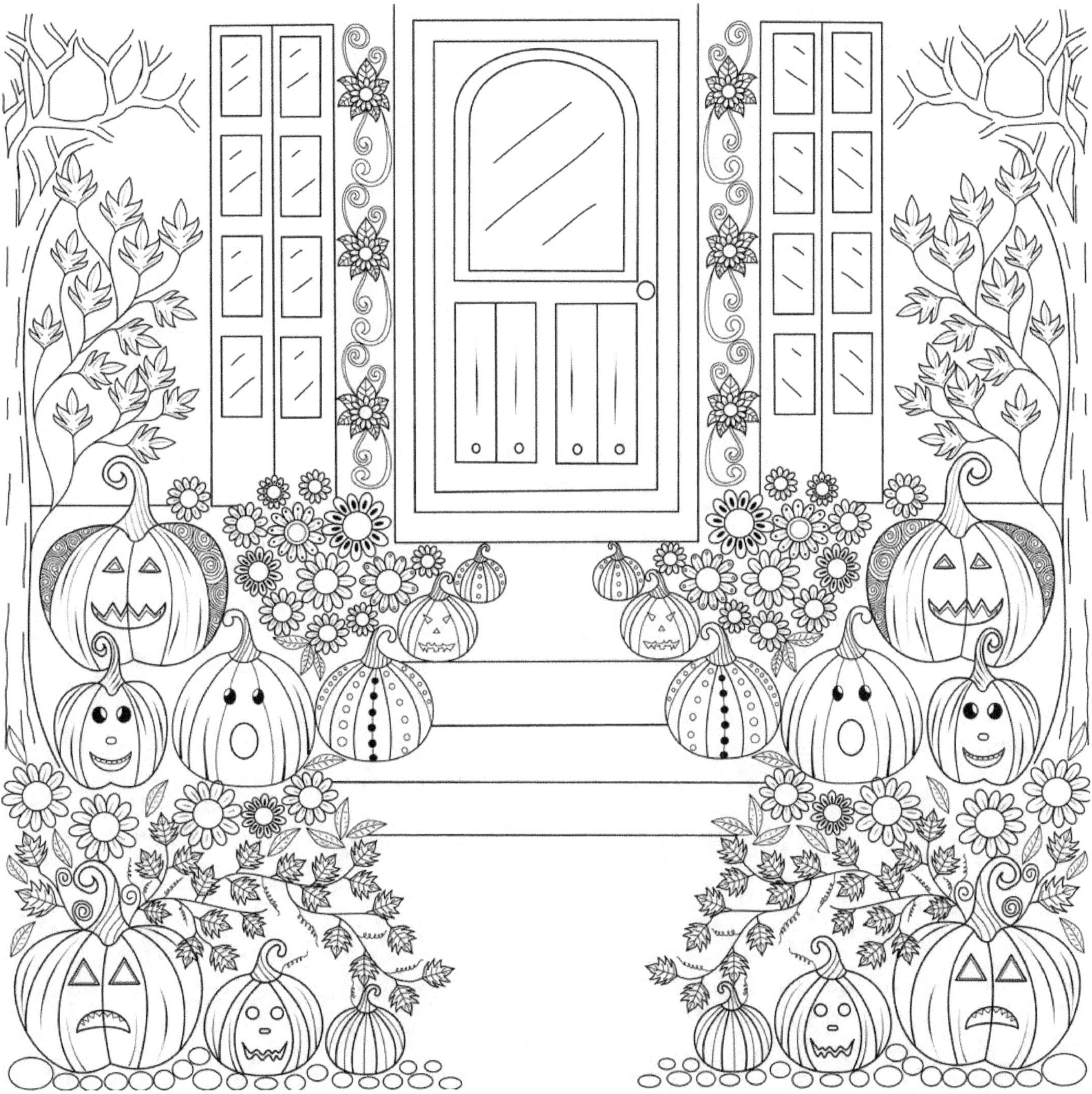

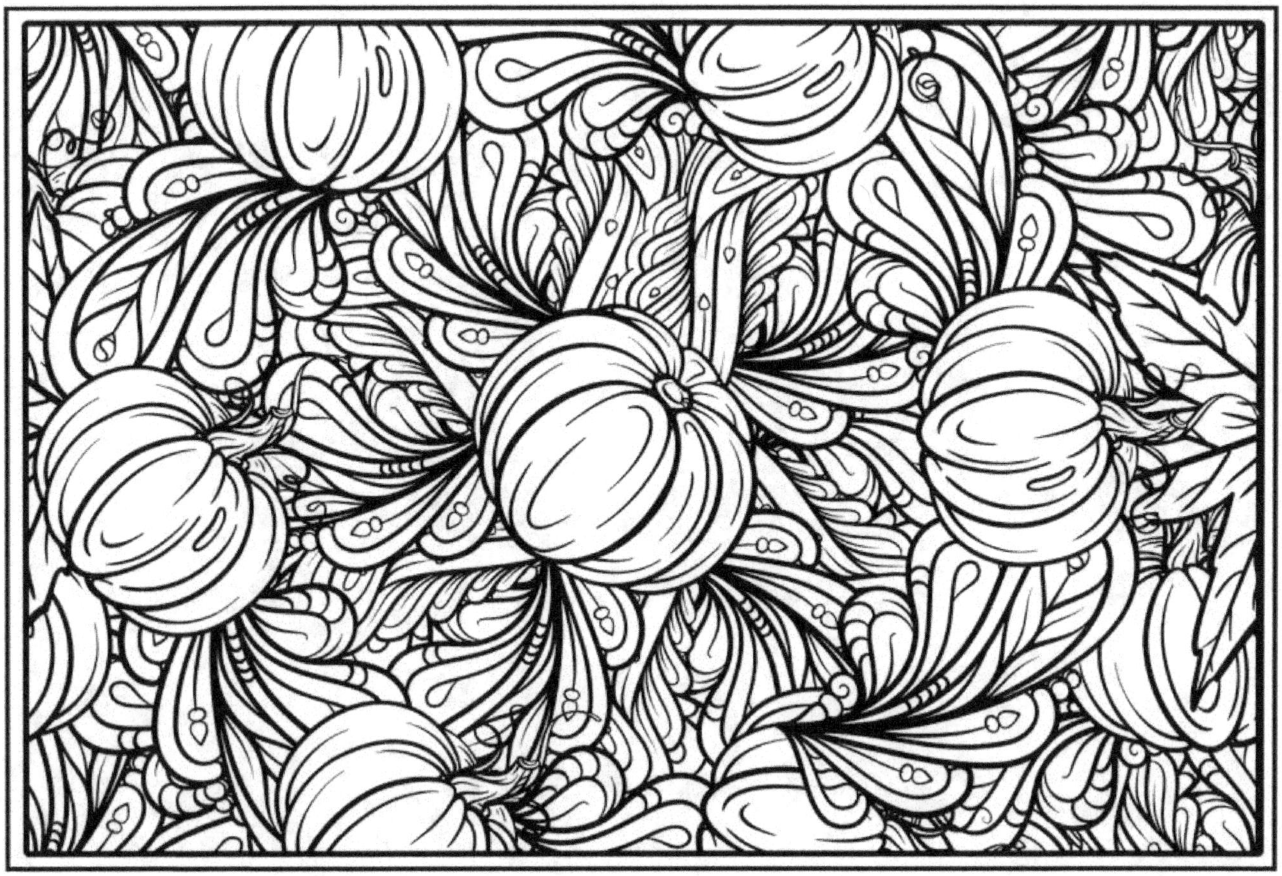

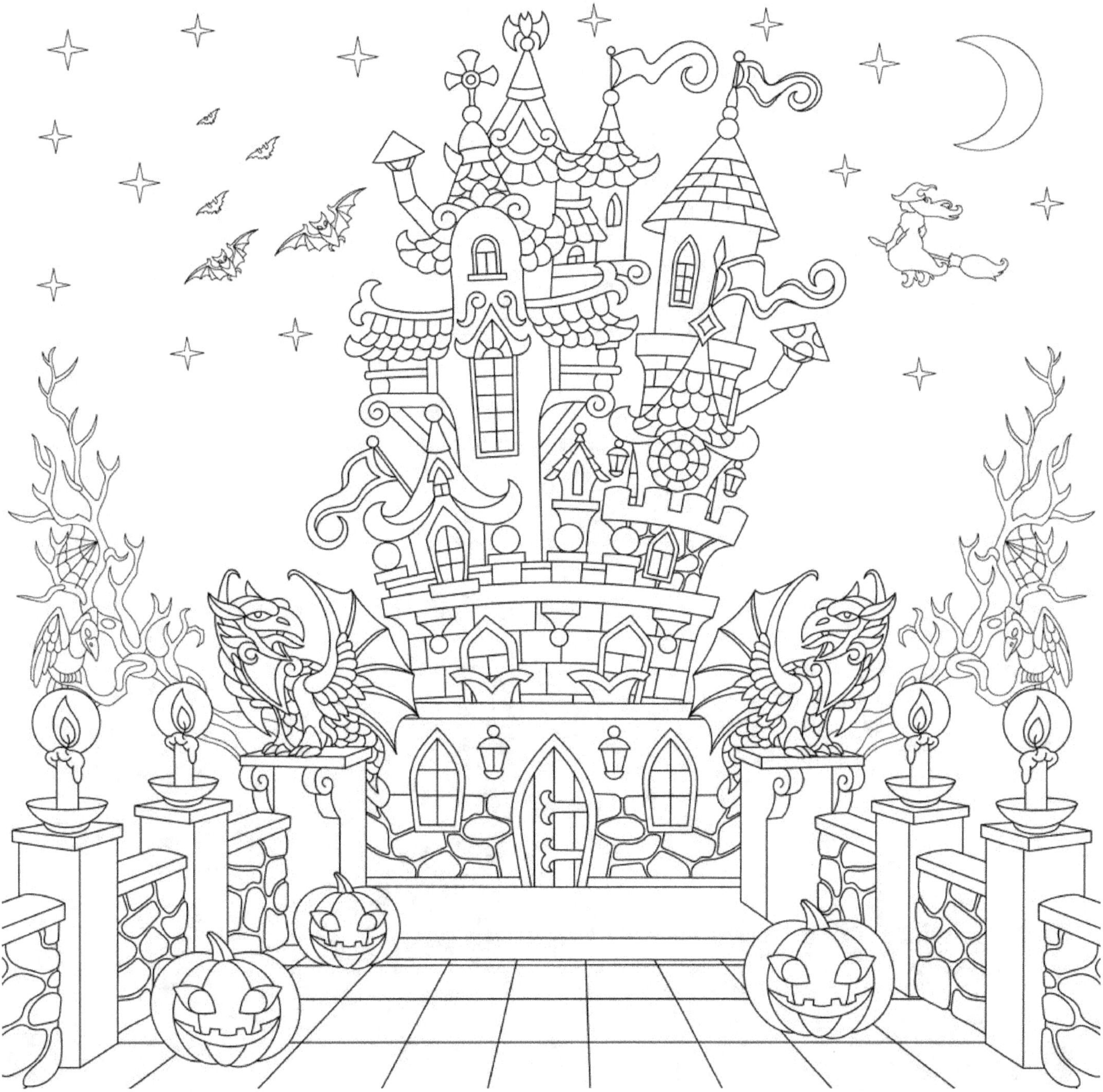

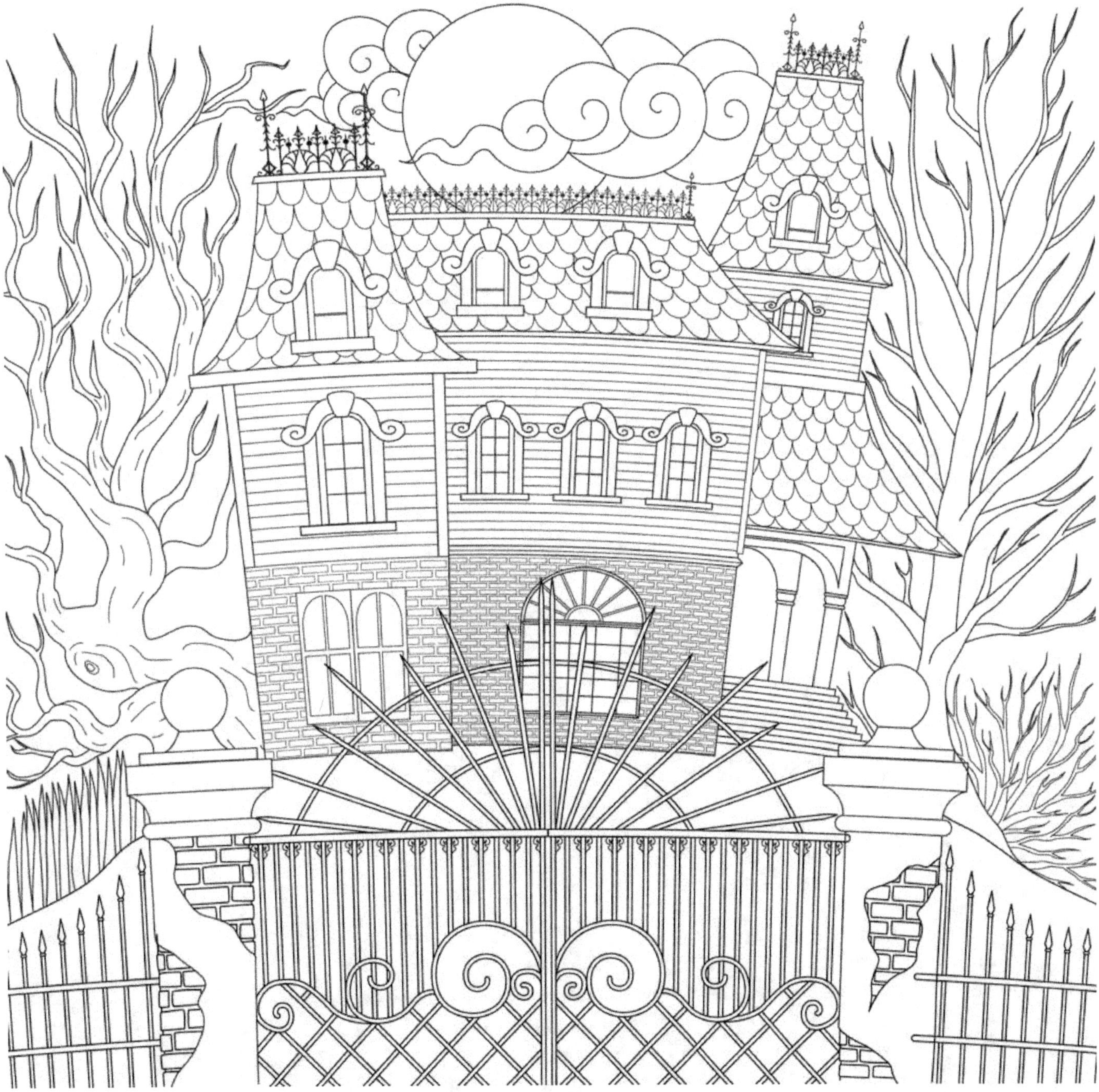

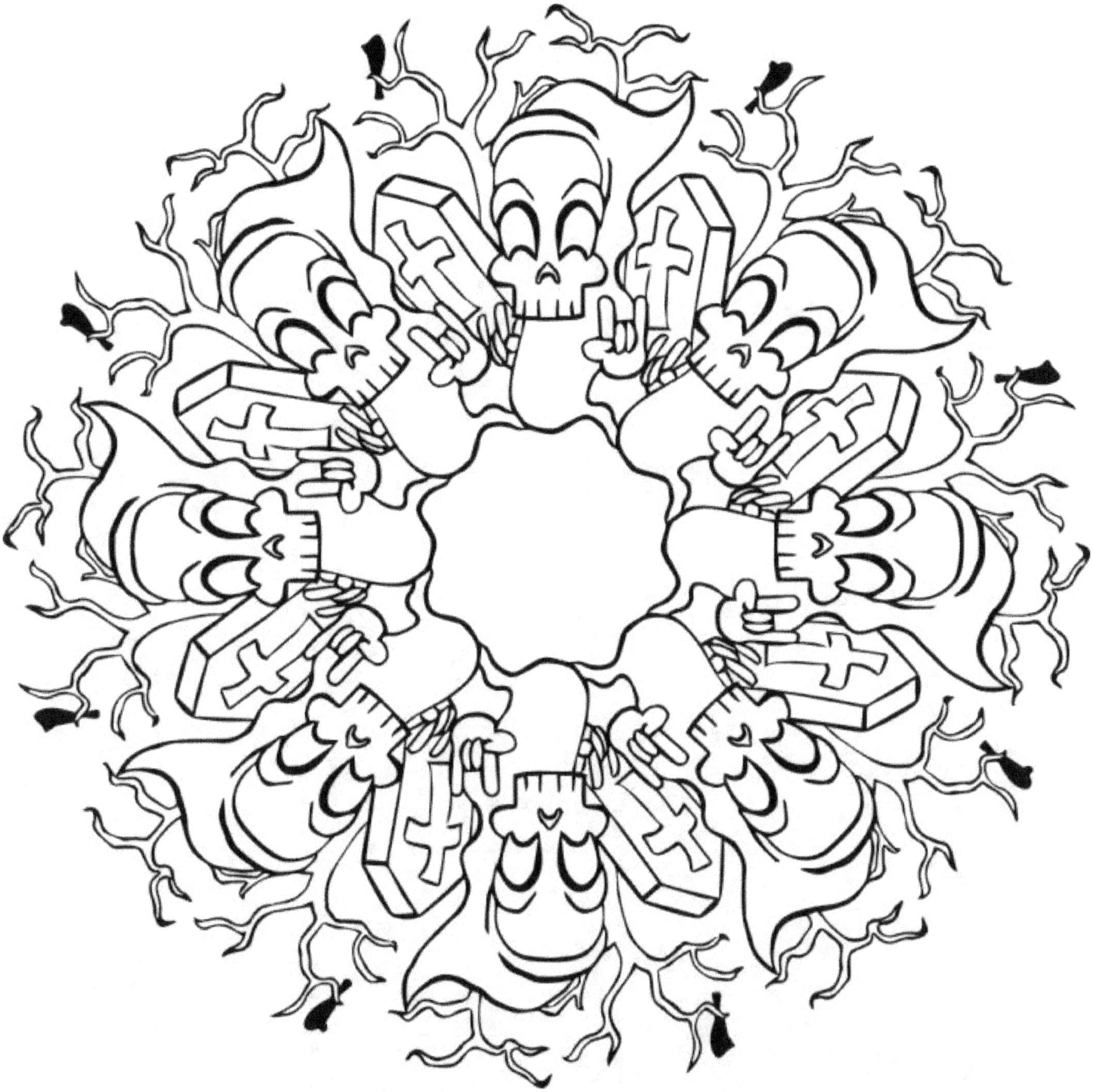

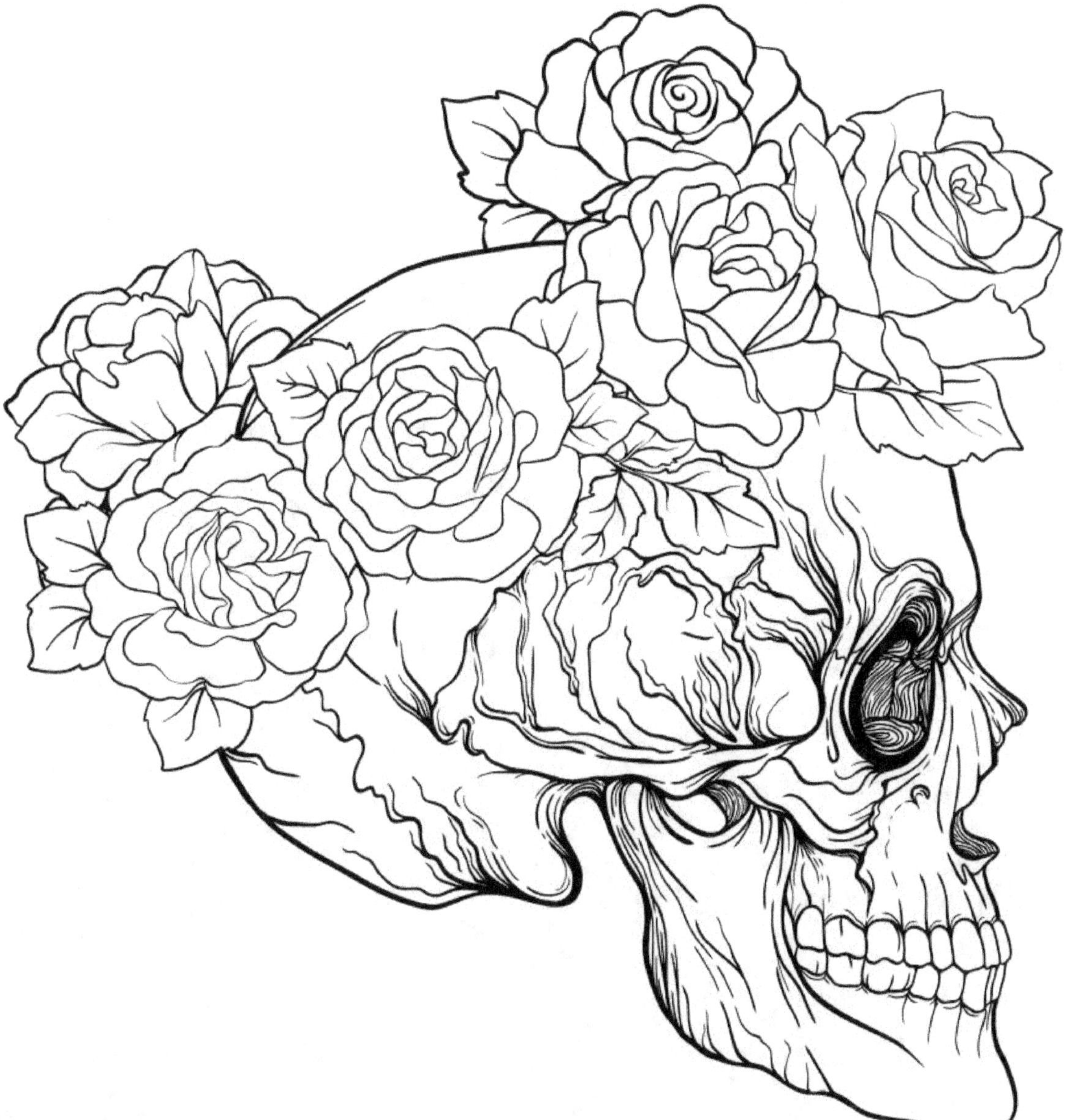

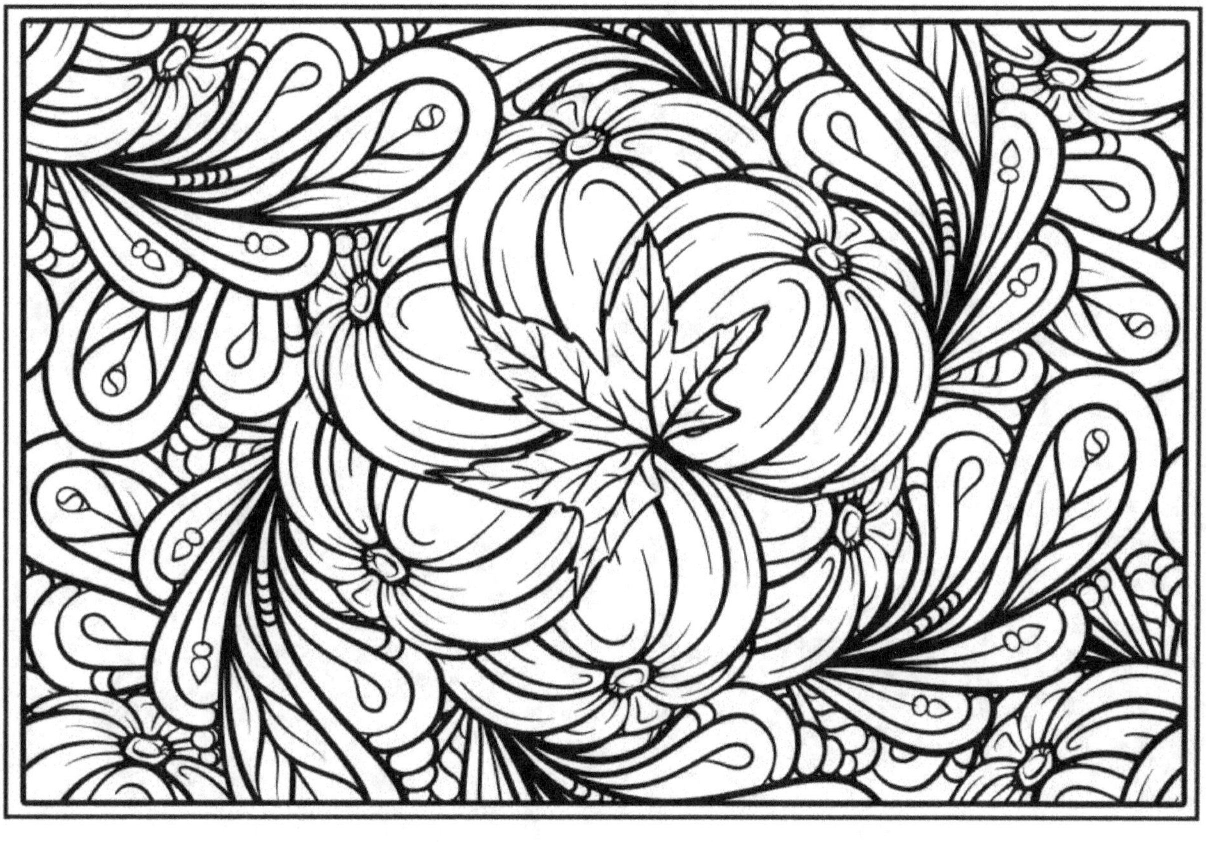

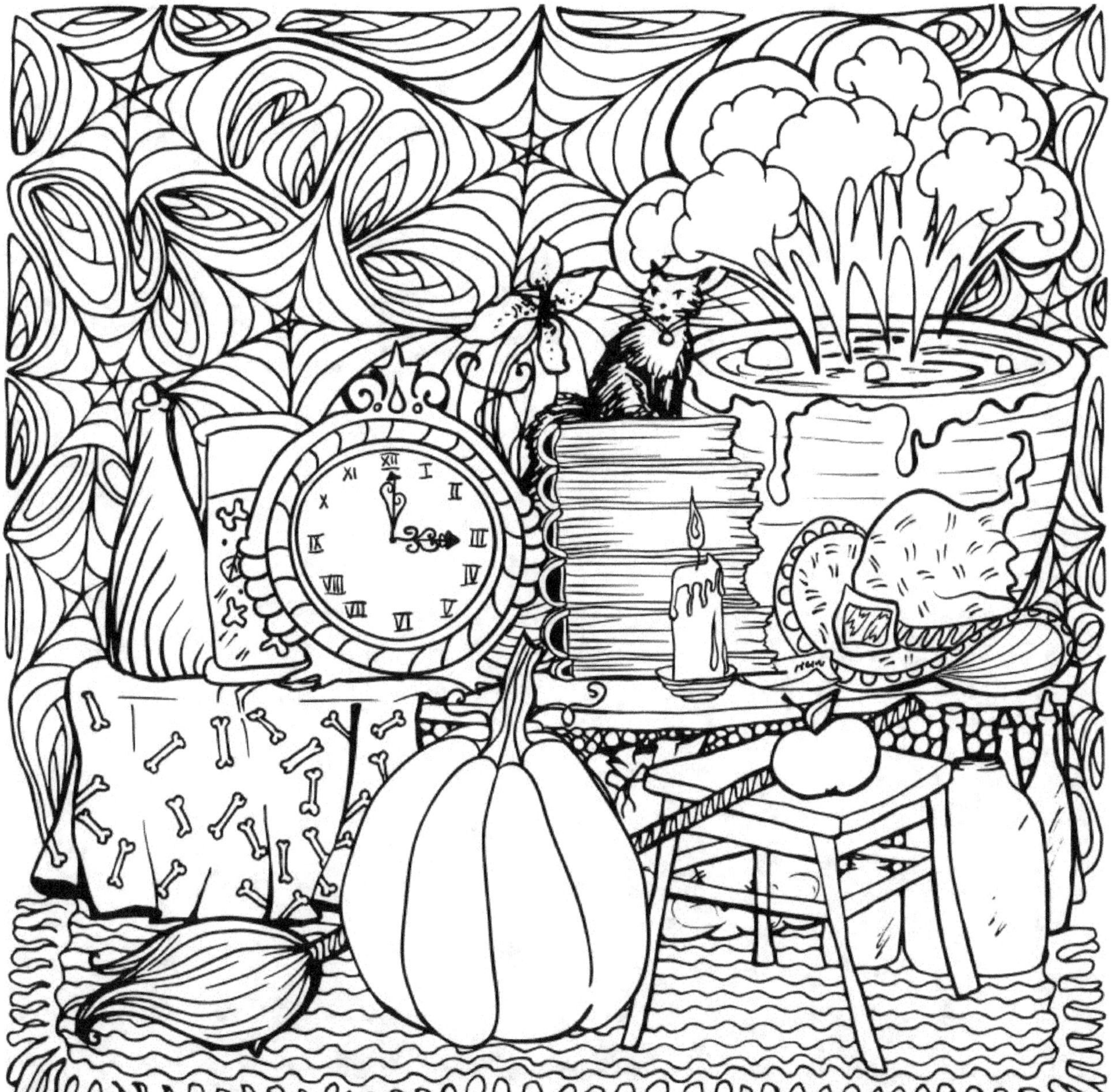

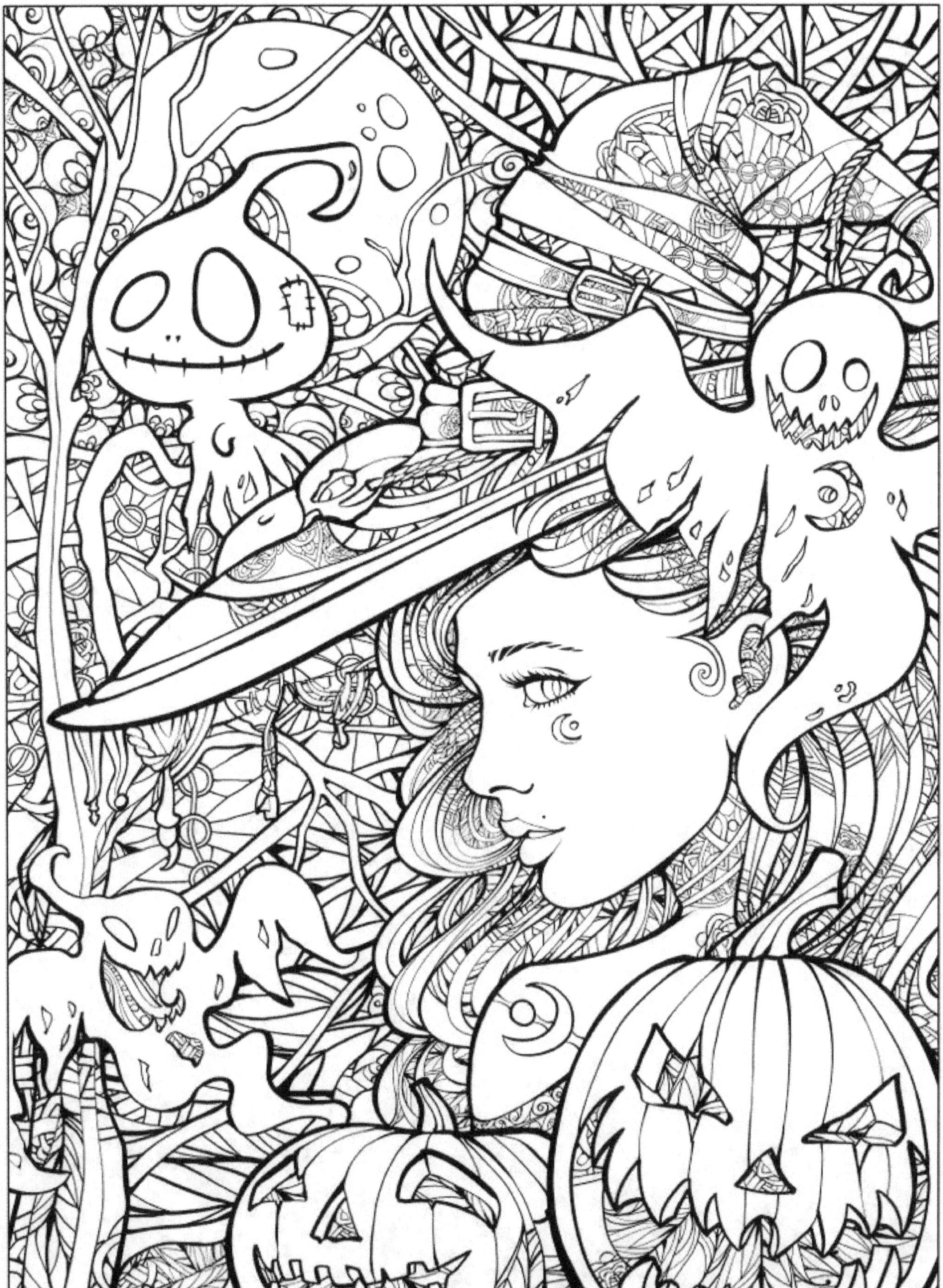

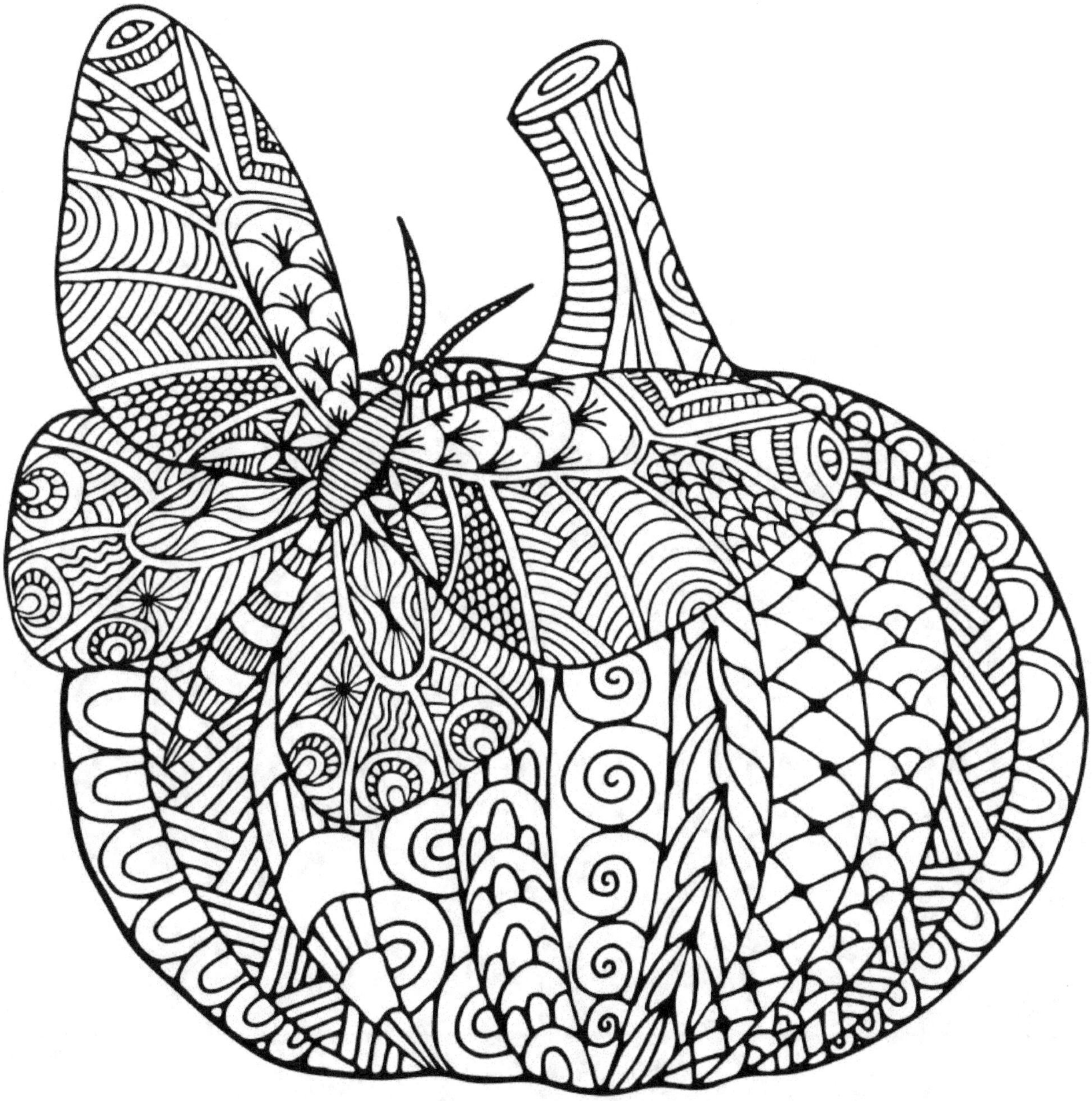

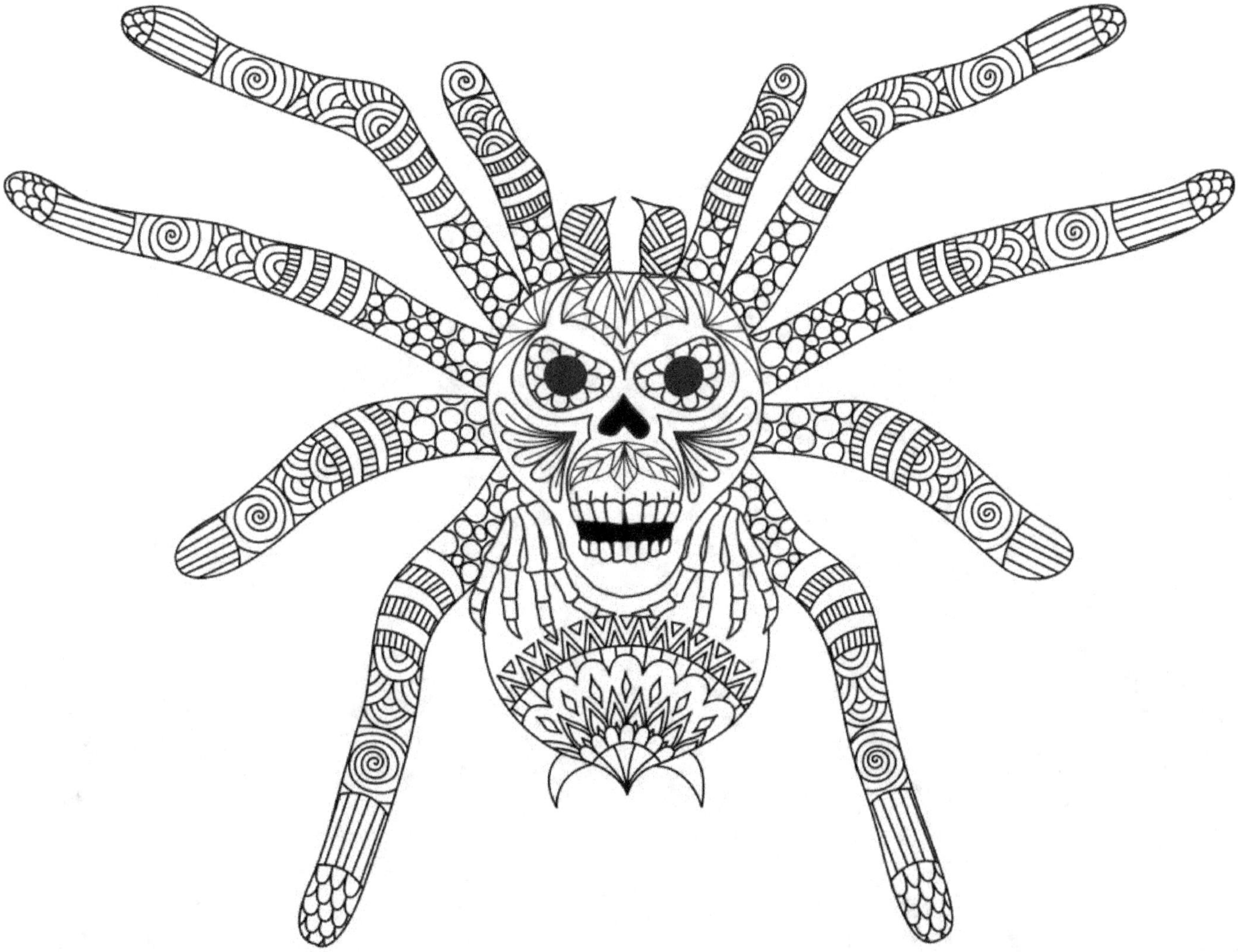

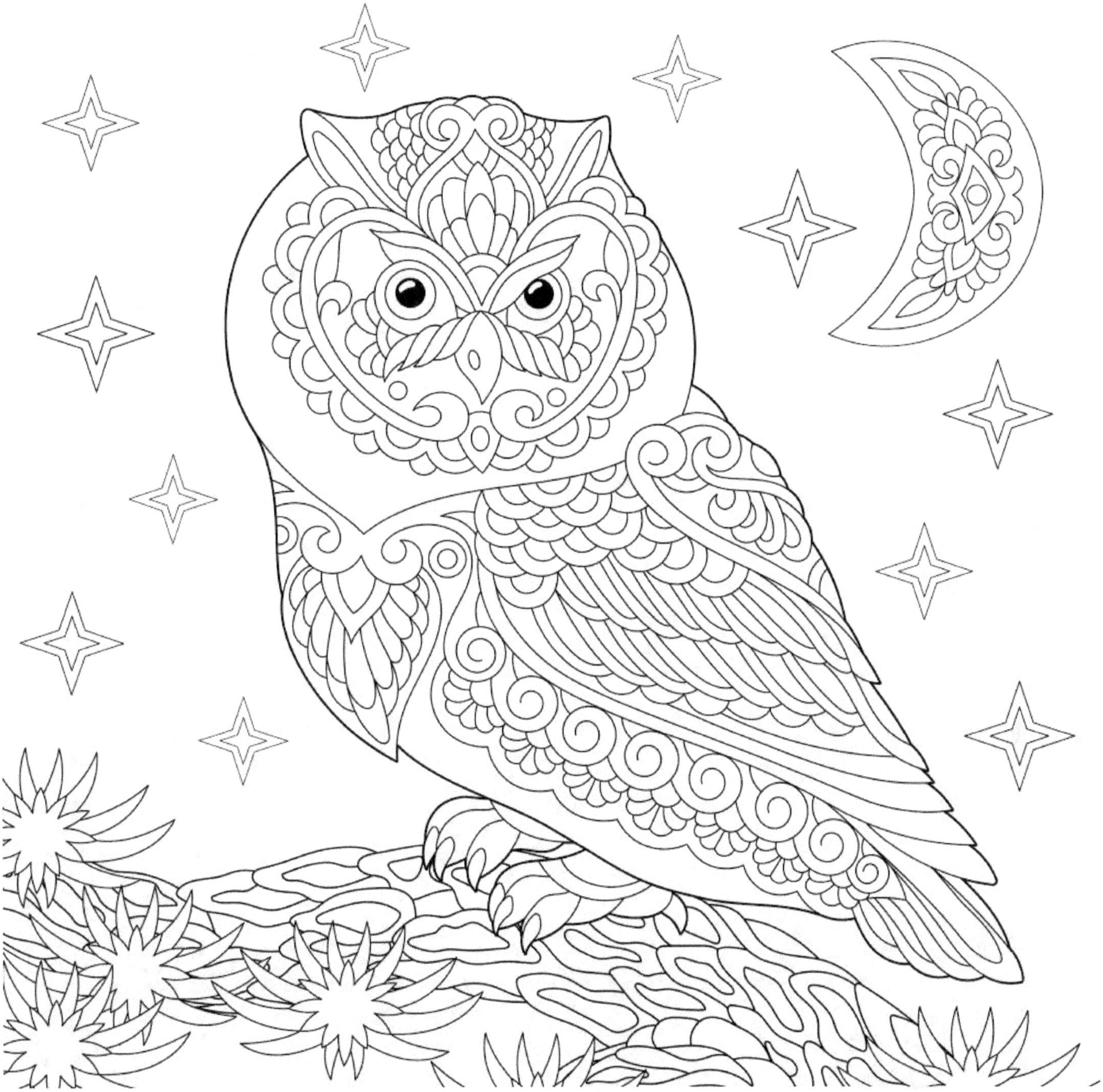

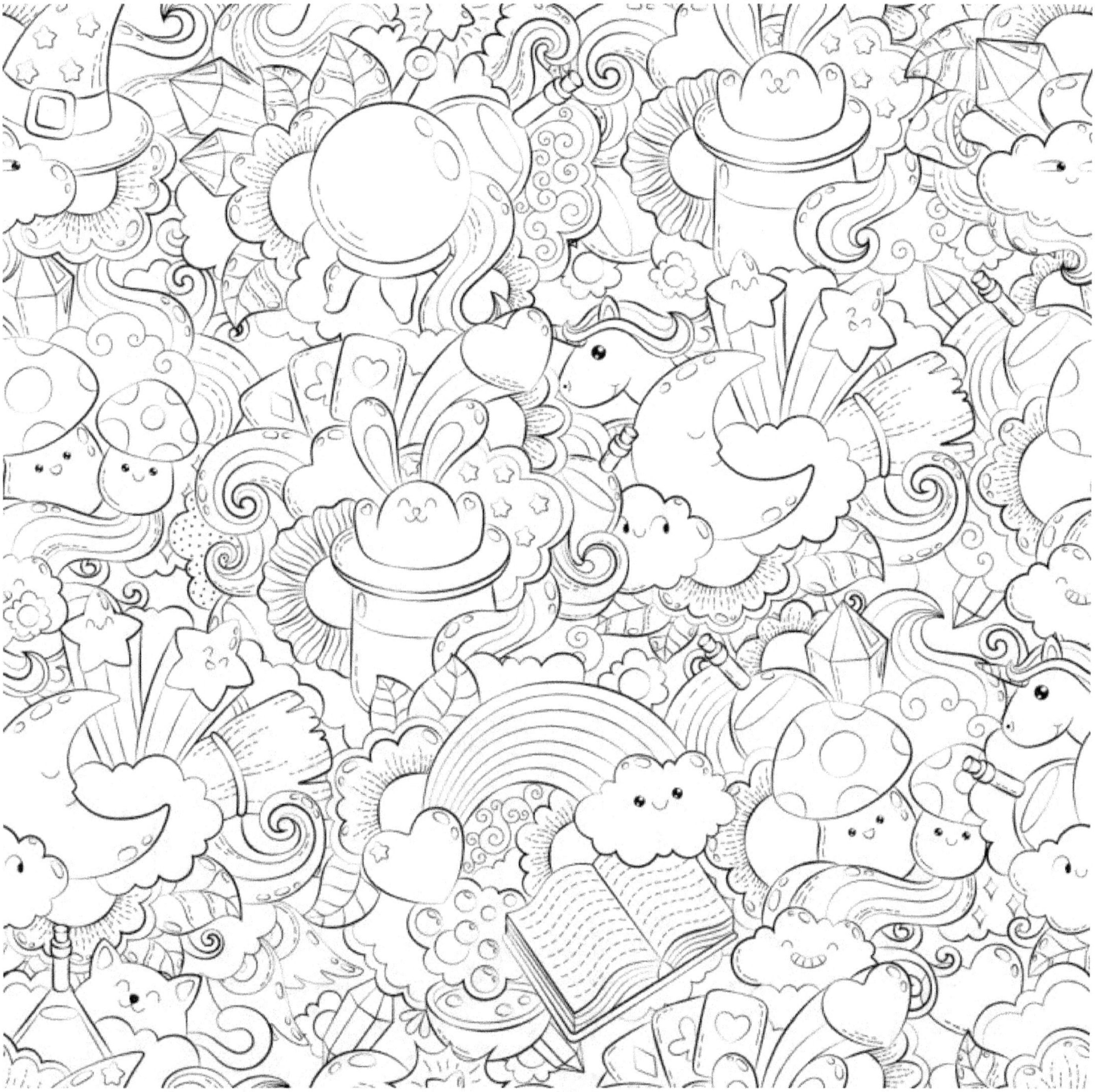

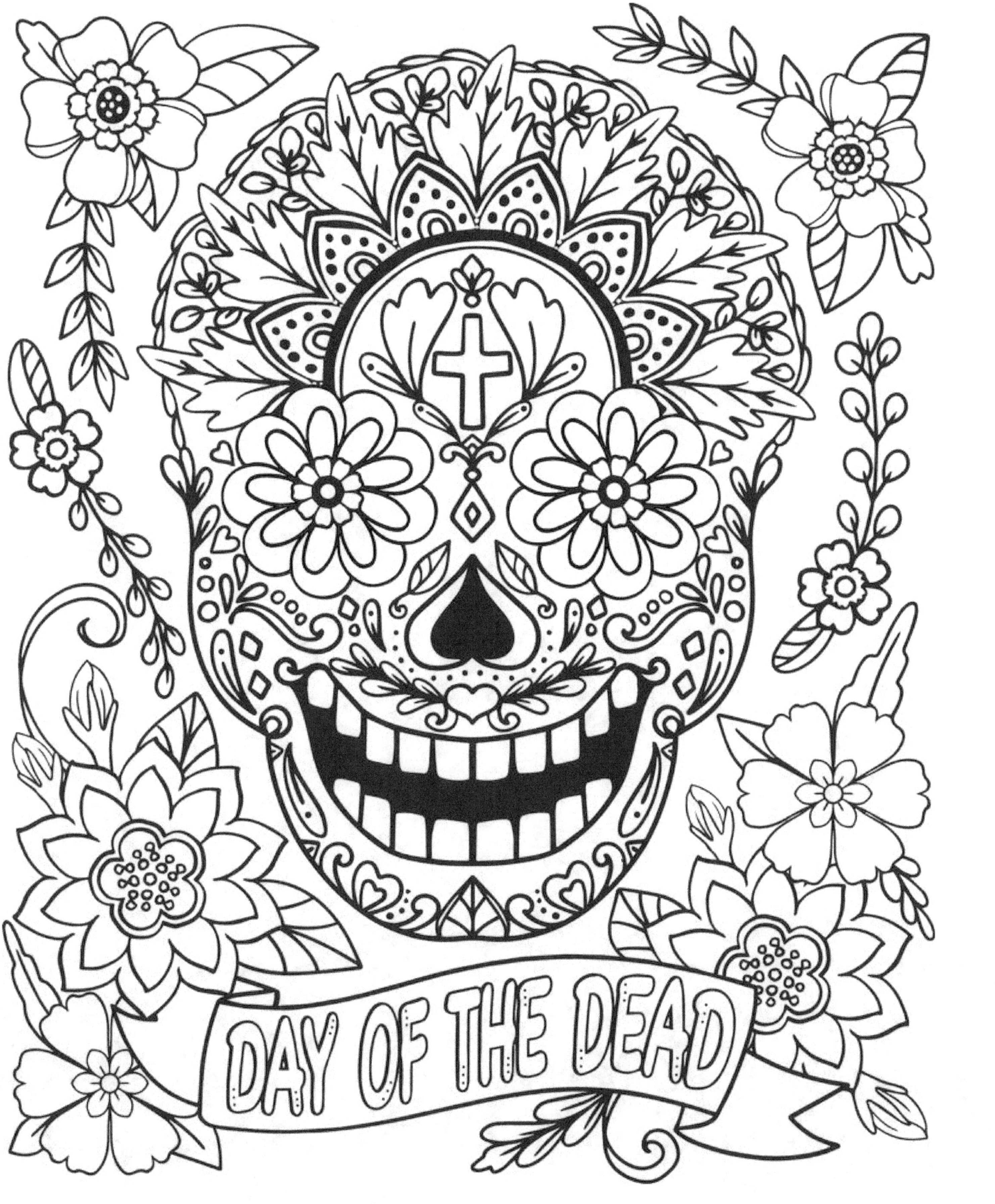
DAY OF THE DEAD

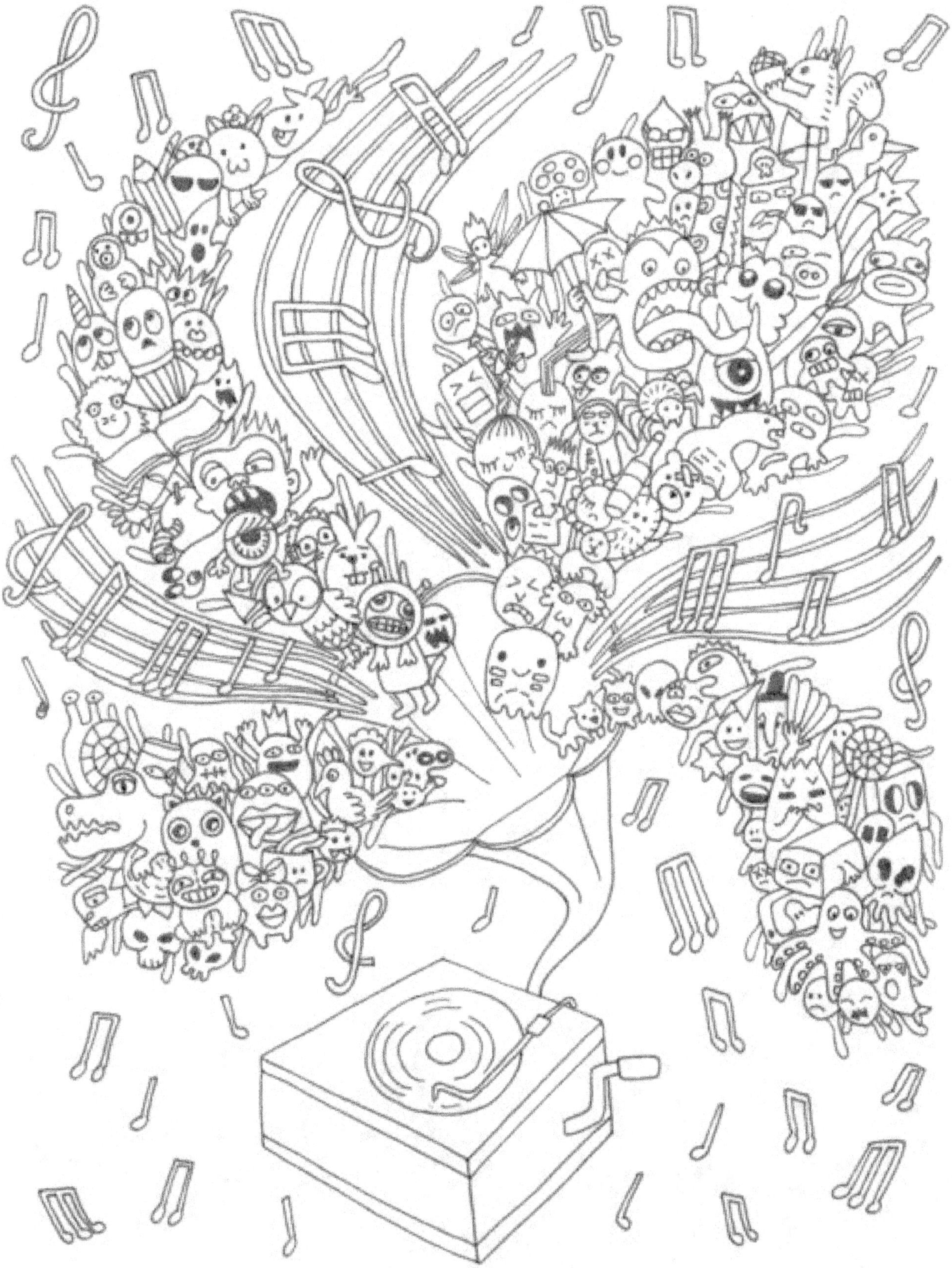

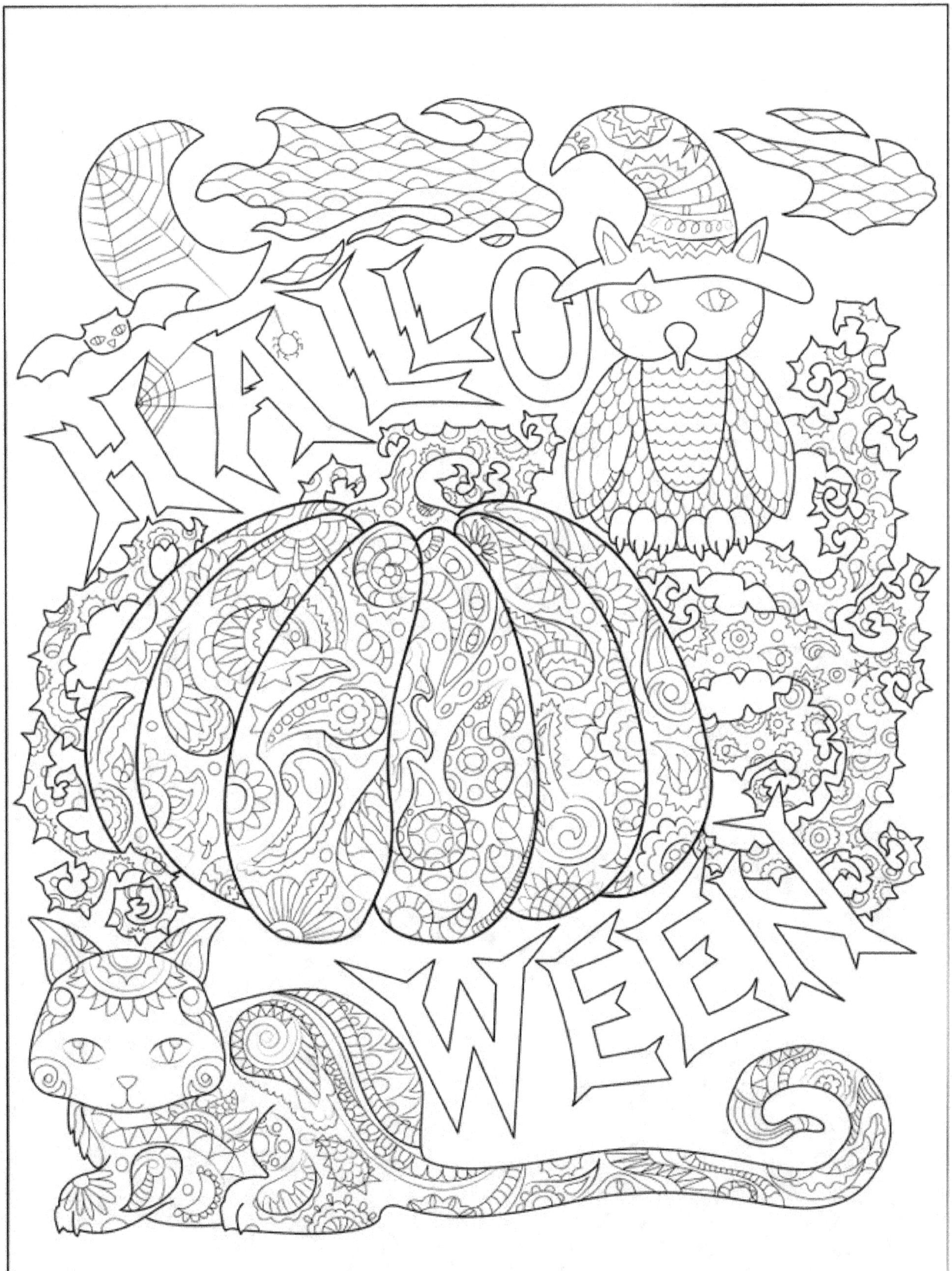
HALLO
WEEN

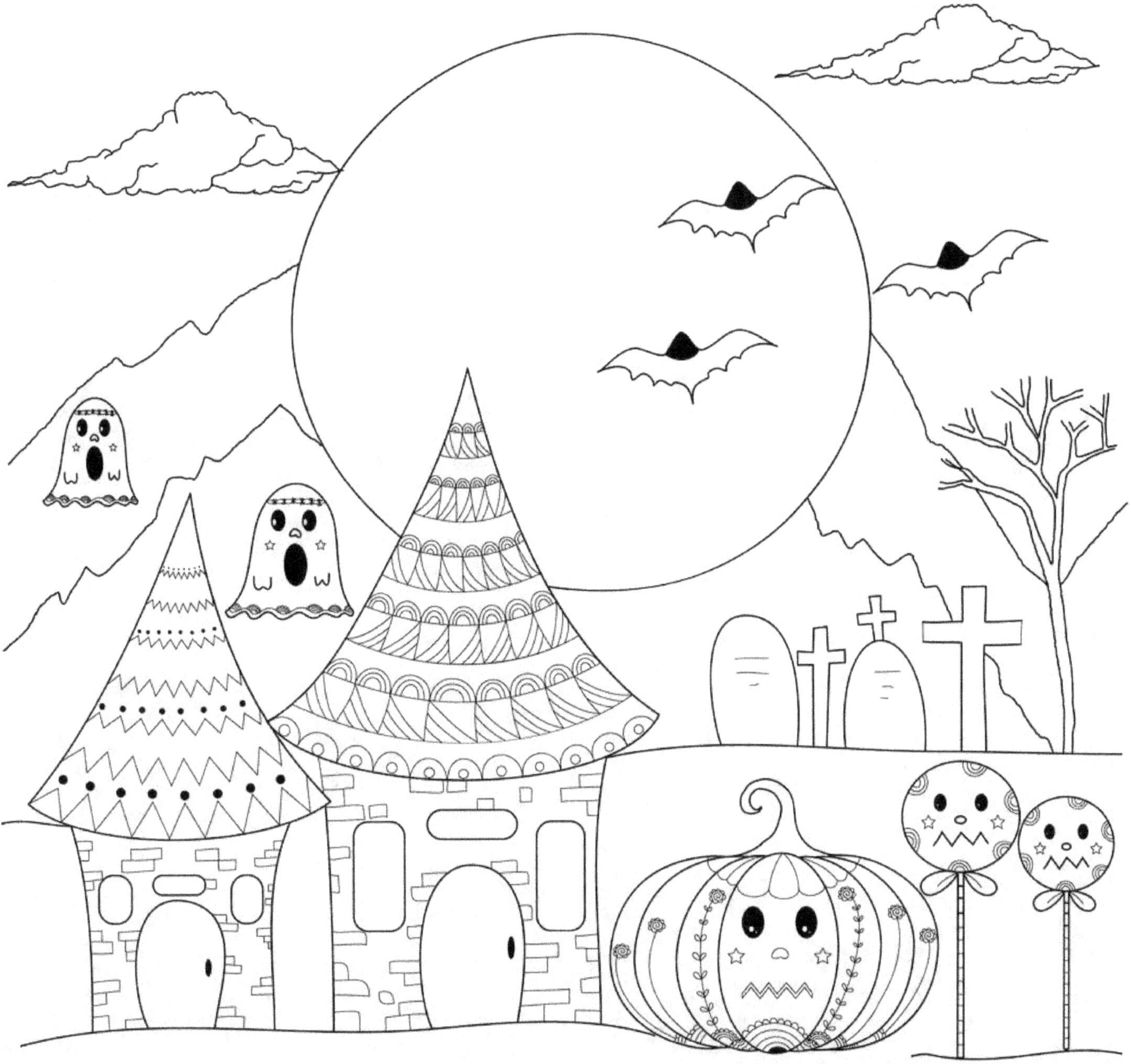

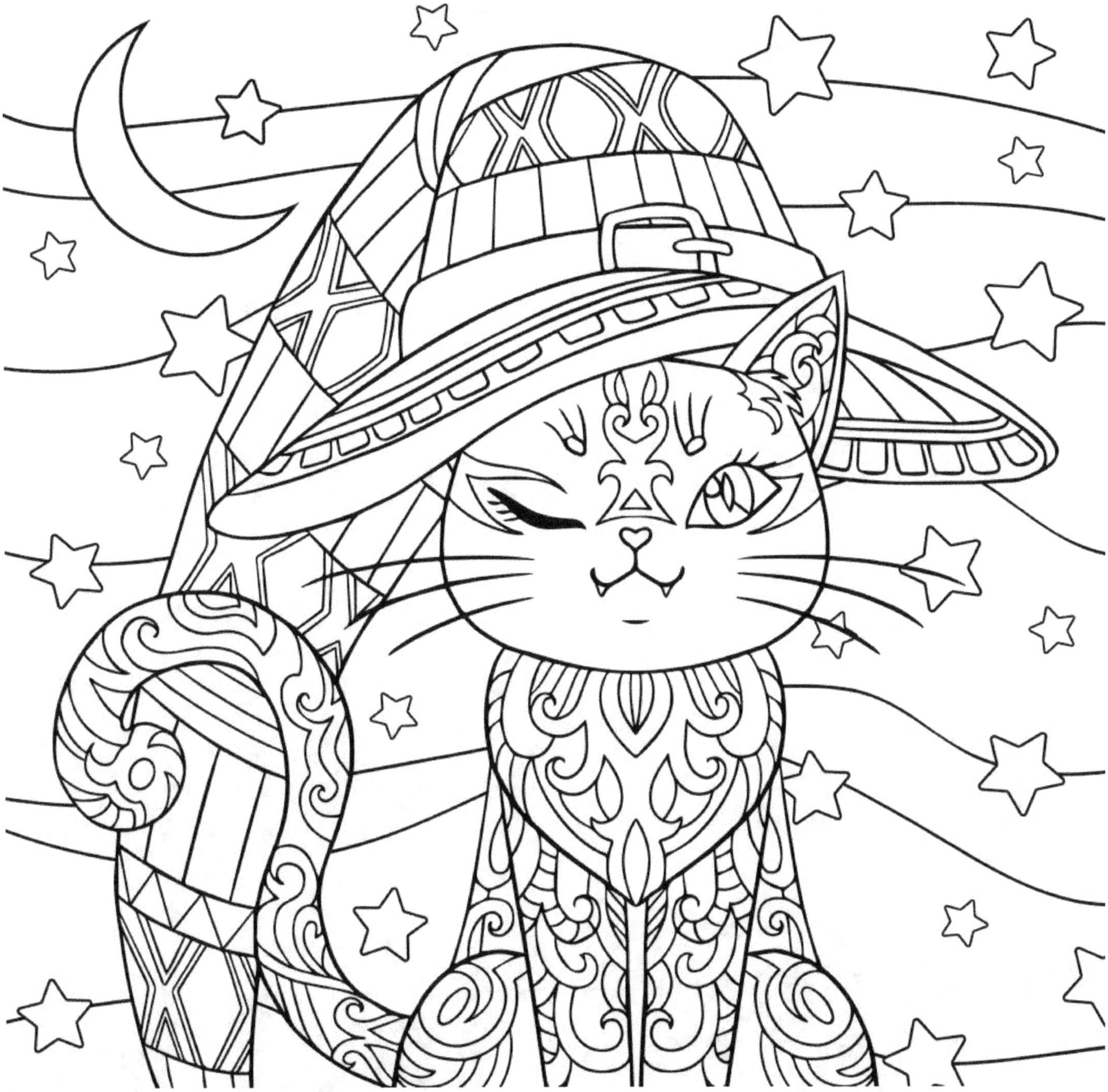

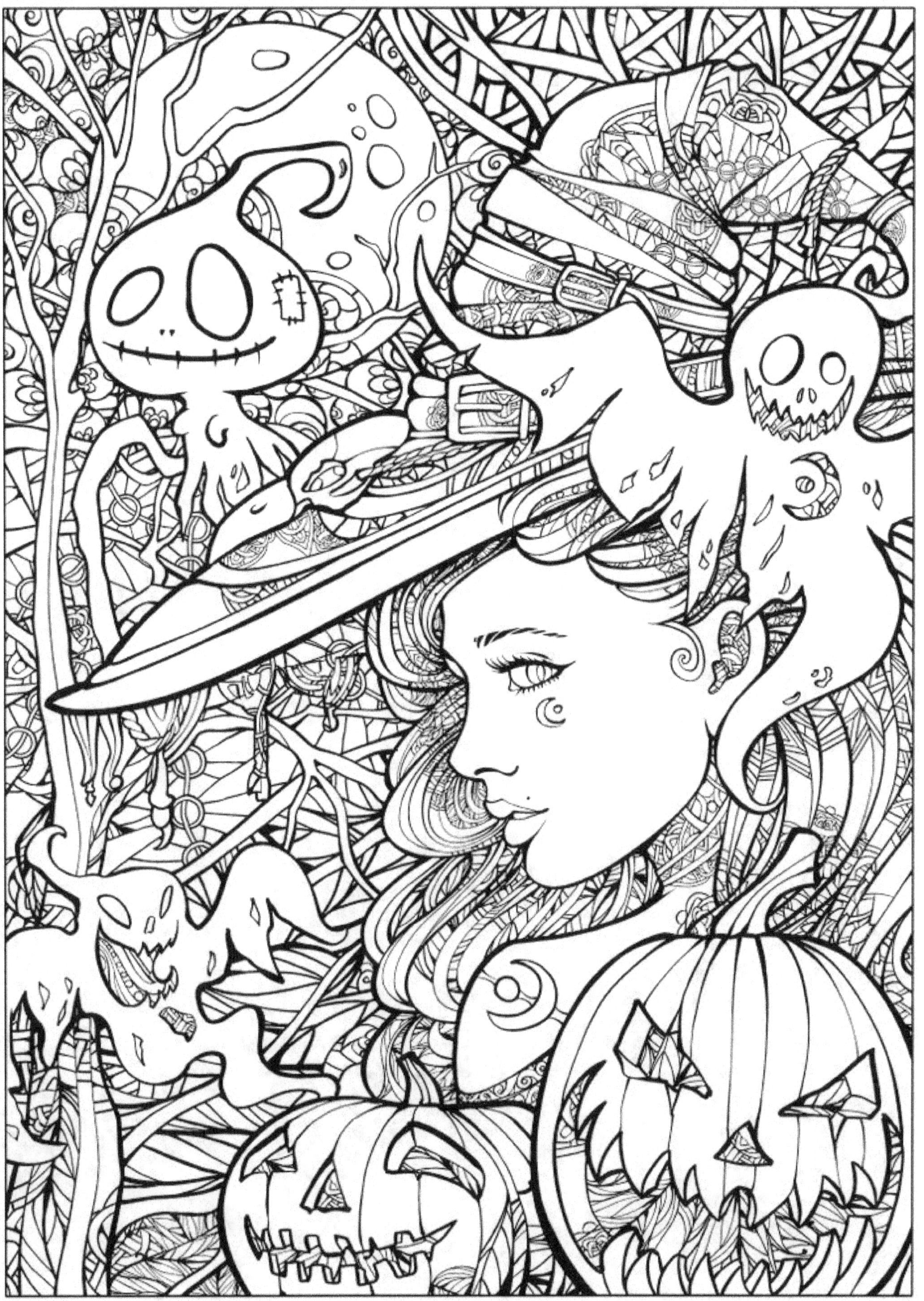

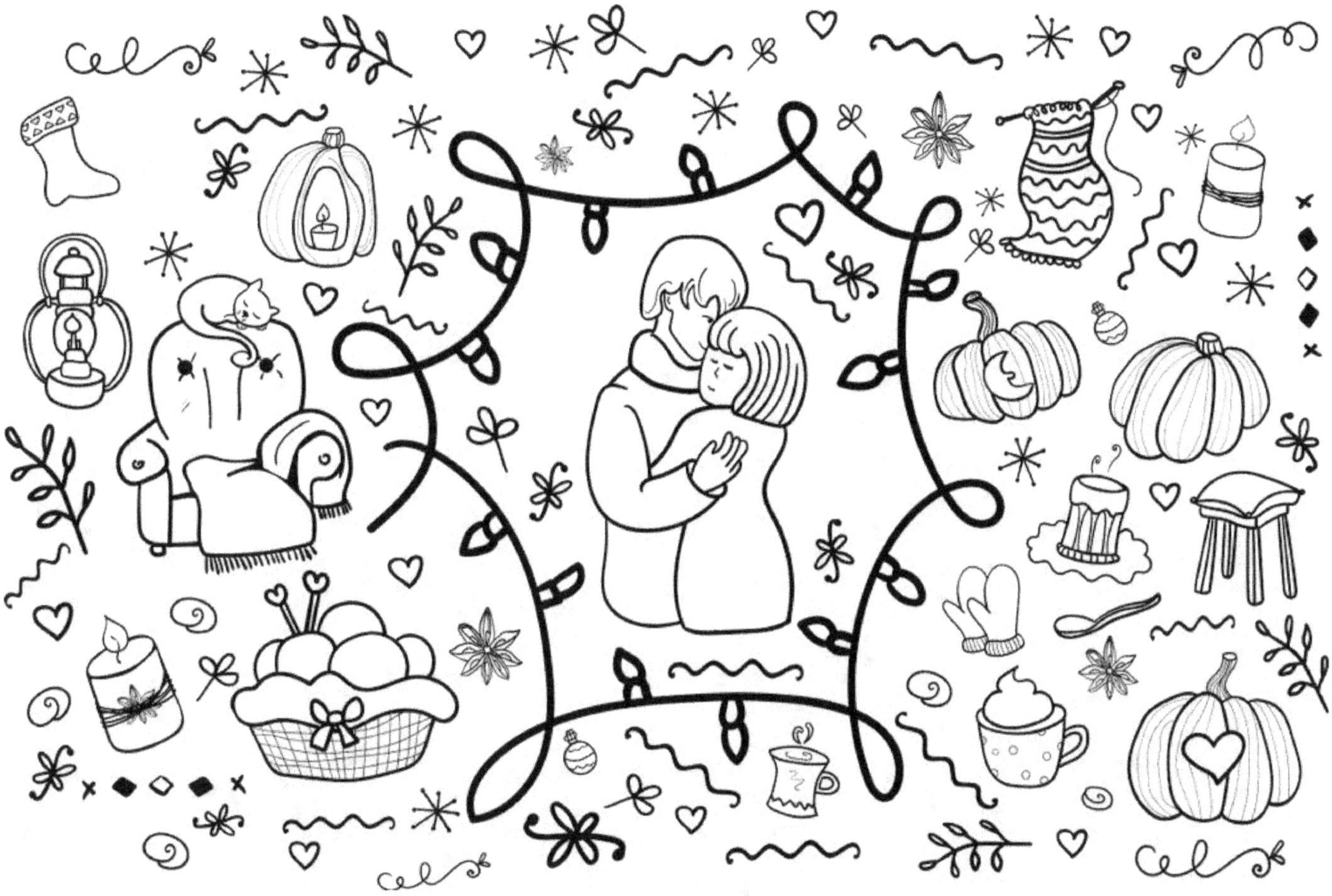

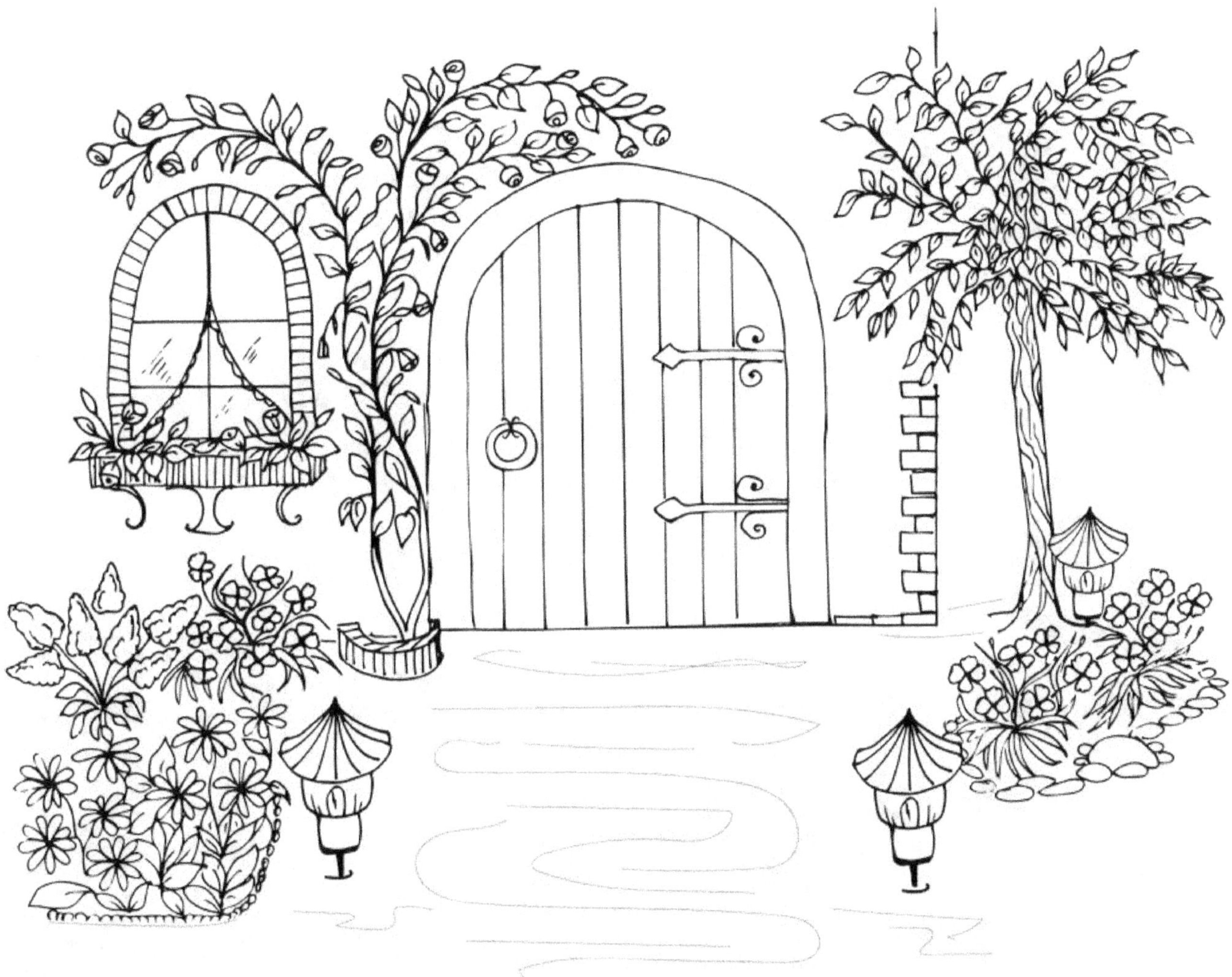

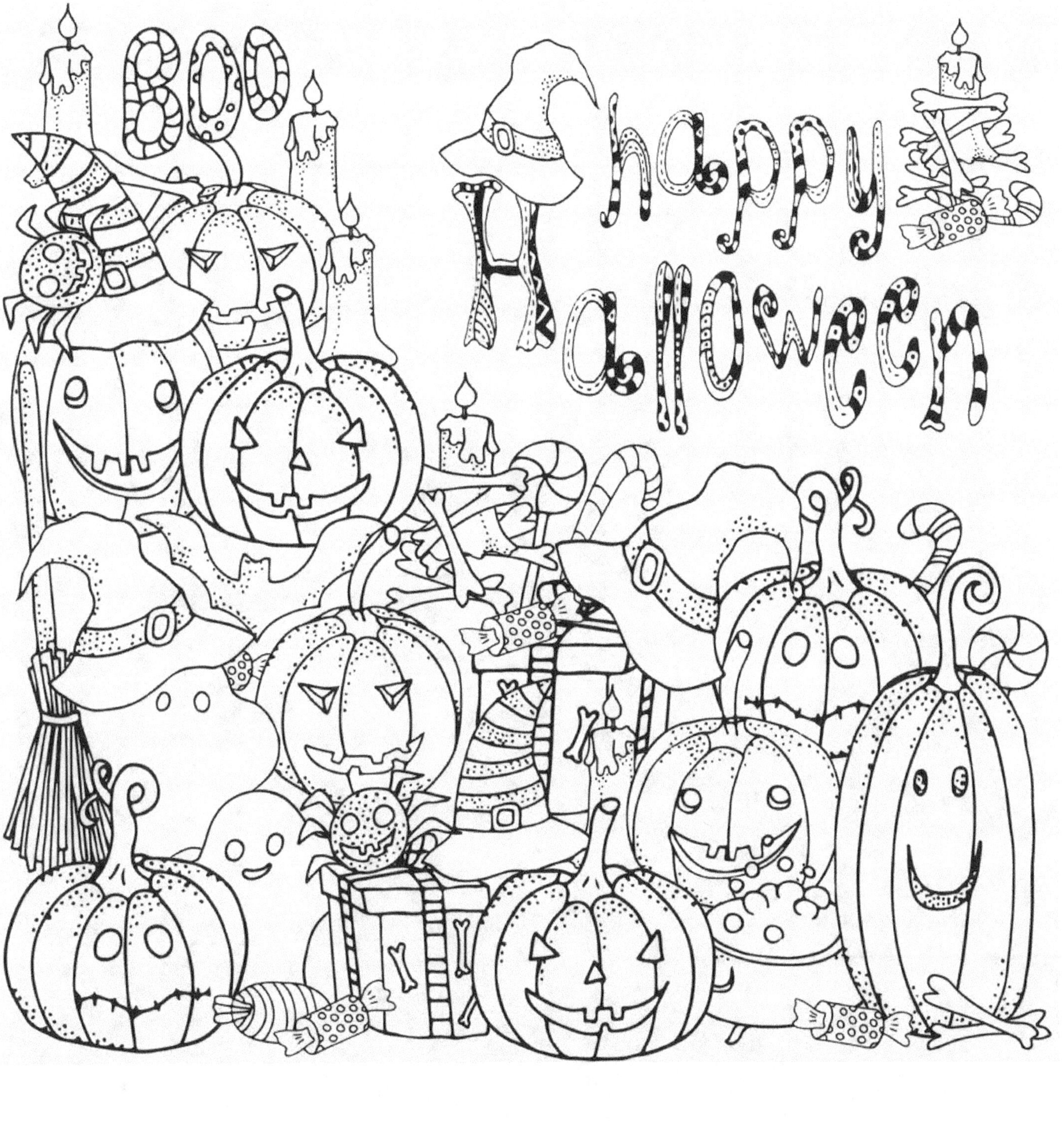
BOO
happy Halloween

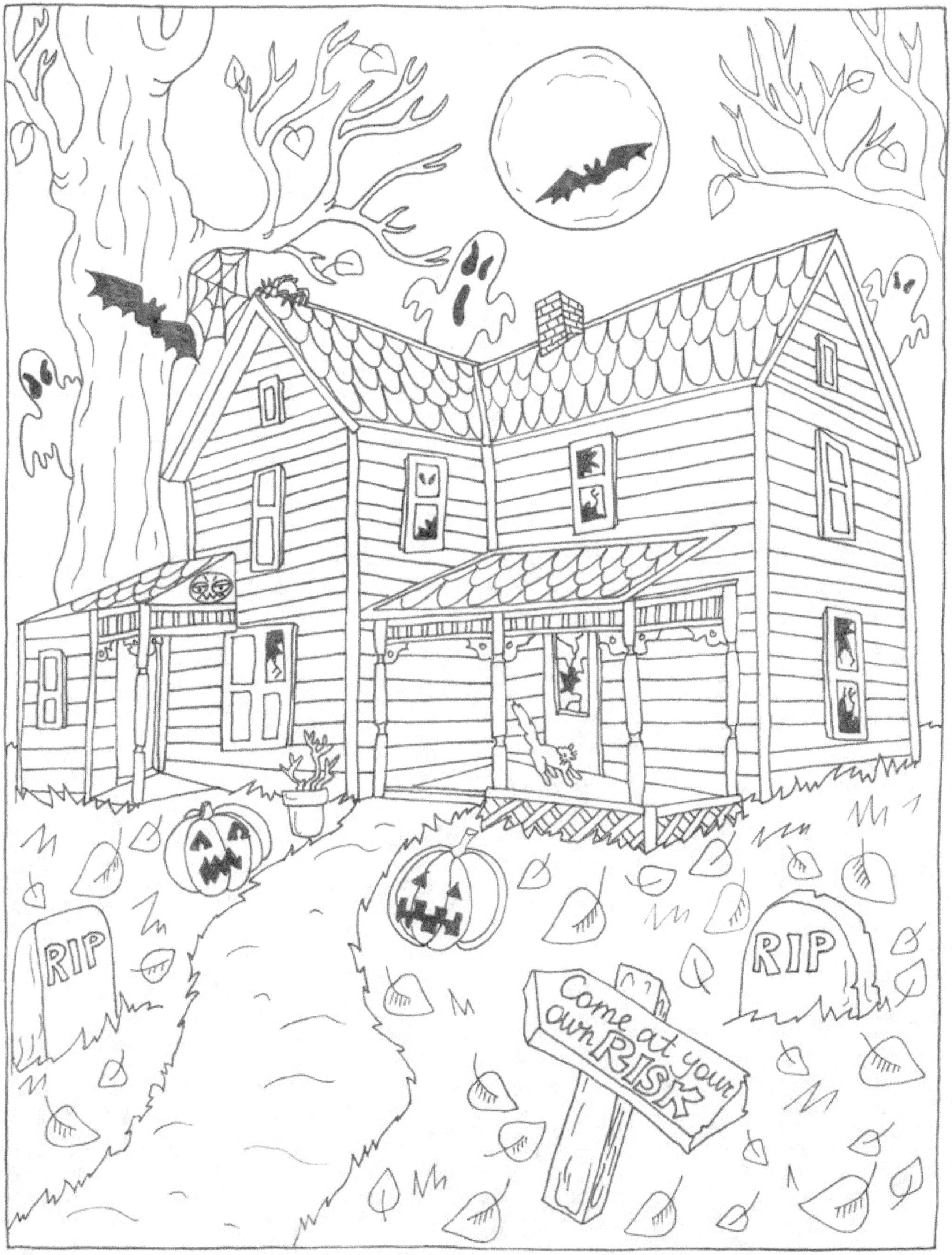
RIP
RIP
Come at your own RISK

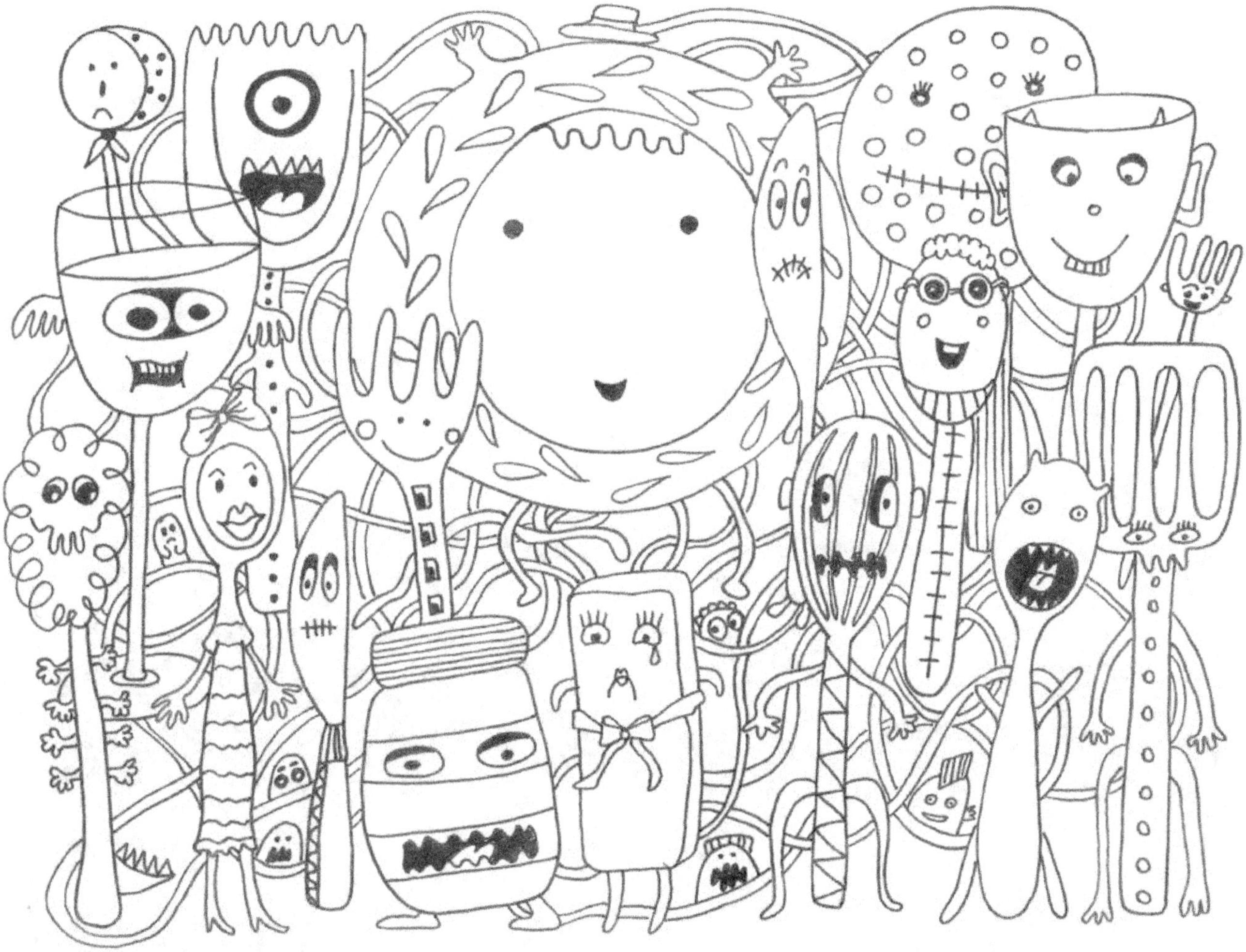

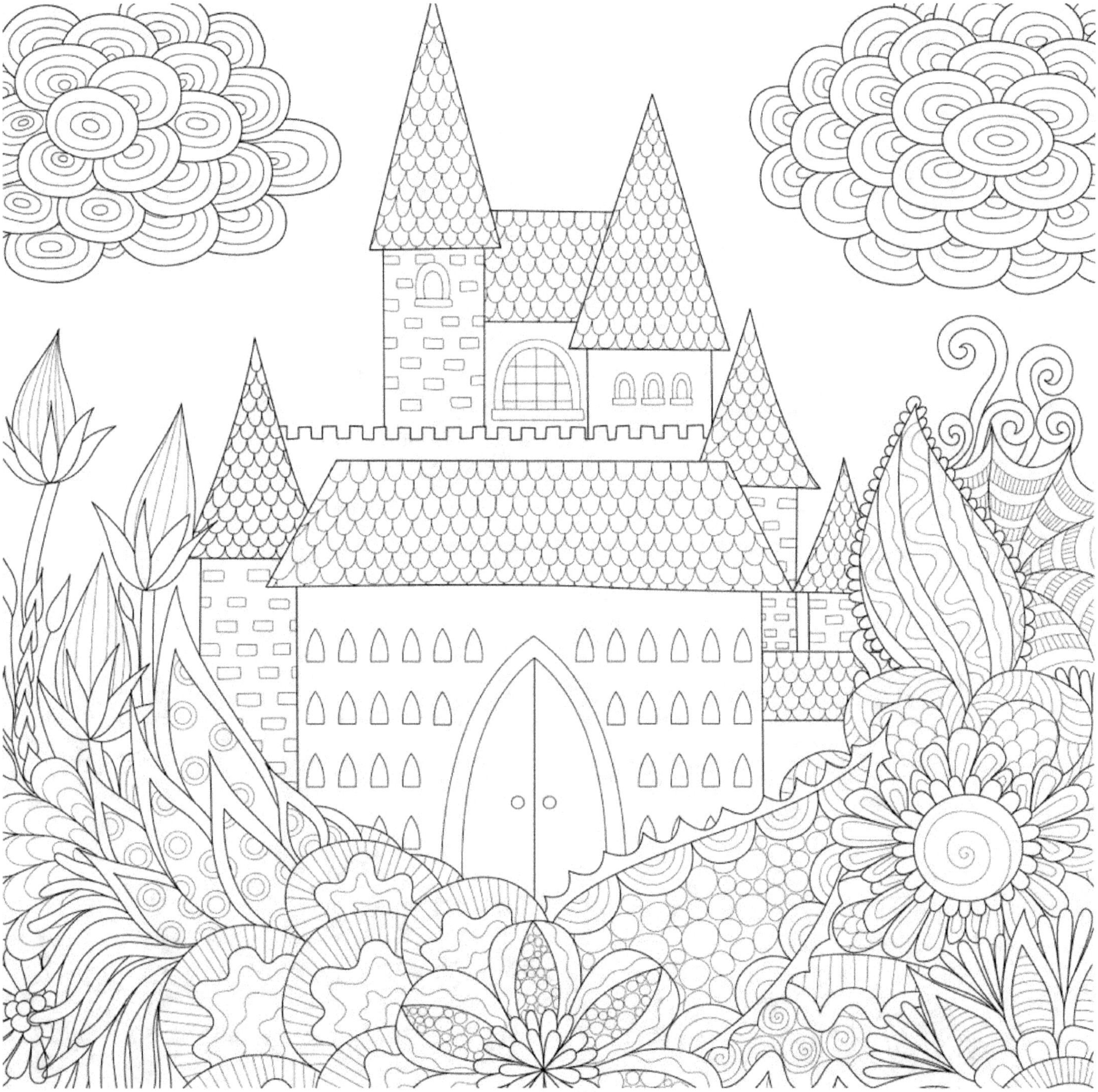

www.ingramcontent.com/pod-product-compliance
Lightning Source LLC
Chambersburg PA
CBHW081524220526
45467CB00010B/3033
* 9 7 9 8 6 8 7 5 4 4 4 2 9 *